Trade Fair Design
Annual 2000

Messedesign
Jahrbuch 2000

International

Conway Lloyd Morgan

Trade Fair Design Annual 2000

Messedesign Jahrbuch 2000

International

avedition

Contents

Inhaltsverzeichnis

What Virtual Future?

Wo liegt die virtuelle Zukunft?

Ralph Grabowski's Upfront e-zine is a creation of the Internet: a weekly compendium of news on CAD programs, market developments and product reviews. It's a one person enterprise read around the world, distributed on the Internet and only possible because of that. He recently asked whether trade shows would survive, given the ability of the Internet and the World Wide Web to deliver information continuously and regardless of geography. A few years ago Clement Mok, one of the creators of the Apple Computer, suggested to a friend that the new technologies would make the trade fair redundant. It is a notion that one still hears quite often. So in the year 2000 should we be looking at the end of the trade fair? The idea of the modern fair dates back to Prince Albert's notion of an international manufacturing celebration, which became the Great Exhibition in London of 1851. One hundred and fifty years later, is the idea still a valid one?

The answer would seem to be yes, on the present evidence. There are several aspects to this. Firstly, many of the major international fairs are attracting larger exhibitor investment and maintaining or increasing visitor numbers. (Indeed, the new information technology and computing world, far from ending the trade fair, itself revolves around several major fairs, including CeBIT in Germany and Comdex and Siggraph in the USA.) Secondly, what the proponents of the Internet as interface forget is that fairs have a human dimension. We don't only visit them to look at new products and place orders, but to meet colleagues, rivals, friends, to put names to faces, and to get the feedback feeling of being there. The chance to compare different products, to get a "hands-on" appreciation of what is on show, is too important to miss. Thirdly, we have all learnt from computing the value of redundancy, in the sense of having different ways of accessing the same infor-mation. And website managers are themselves looking at trade fair design. One problem with e-commerce sites, for example, is the number of visitors who give up halfway through a purchase and leave, so one design group is looking at traffic patterns on stands to see if there are lessons about intervention points to be learned from them. These and similar practices suggest that the trade fair is maintaining its role. This does not mean that stand designers can ignore the Internet and the World Wide Web. Many are already adding terminals to stands, so that data from websites or intranets can be accessed by visitors.

Ralph Grabowskis E-Magazin „Upfront" verdankt seine Entstehung dem Internet: wöchentlich liefert es eine Zusammenstellung von Neuheiten im Zusammenhang mit CAD Programmen, Marktentwicklungen und Produktbeurteilungen. Es ist ein Einmann-Unternehmen, wird weltweit gelesen und über das Internet verbreitet. Kürzlich stellte Ralph Grabowski die Frage, ob Messen überlebensfähig seien – in Anbetracht der Möglichkeiten des Internet und des World Wide Web, Informationen permanent und global zu liefern. Schon ein paar Jahre vorher erwähnte Clement Mok, einer der Entwickler des Apple Computers, daß die neuen Technologien Messen bald überflüssig machen würden. Diese Ansicht wird auch heute noch oft vertreten. Sollten wir uns deshalb im Jahr 2000 auf das Aus der Messen vorbereiten? Prinz Alberts Idee einer internationalen Feier anläßlich der industriellen Entwicklung, welche zur Weltausstellung in London im Jahre 1851 führte, war die Basis für die moderne Messe. Ist diese Idee, hundertfünfzig Jahre später, noch gültig?

Laut der gegenwärtigen Situation lautet die Antwort ja, diverse Gesichtspunkte sprechen dafür: Erstens ziehen viele der wichtigen internationalen Messen neben höheren Investitionen der Aussteller gleichbleibende oder sogar steigende Besucherzahlen an. (Tatsächlich drehen sich – weit entfernt von einem Abwärtstrend – die neuen Informationstechnologien und Computerwissenschaften rund um mehrere große Messen wie die CeBIT in Deutschland und Comdex und Siggraph in den USA.) Zweitens vergessen Befürworter der Schnittstelle Internet, daß Messen eine menschliche Dimension haben. Wir gehen nicht nur hin, um neue Produkte kennenzulernen und Bestellungen aufzugeben, sondern um Kollegen, Wettbewerber und Freunde zu treffen, um Gesichter mit Namen in Verbindung zu bringen und das Gefühl des Dabeiseins zu erleben. Die Chance, unterschiedliche Produkte zu vergleichen und direkt zu erleben, was ausgestellt wird, ist zu wichtig, um verpaßt zu werden. Drittens haben wir alle durch den Computer die Fülle von Möglichkeiten schätzen gelernt, auf unterschiedlichen Wegen zur selben Information zu kommen. Selbst Website Manager schauen sich die Entwürfe von Messeständen an: Ein Problem des E-Commerce sind Kunden, die auf halbem Weg aufgeben und die Website verlassen, ohne etwas zu kaufen. Deshalb schaut sich eine Designgruppe Besucherströme auf Messeständen an, um feststellen ob es Berührungspunkte zum Verhalten im Internet gibt.

Most importantly of all, trade fair stands have escaped from the hierarchies of manufacturing or classifications by nation that were their worst legacy from the tradition of the great exhibitions. Modern fairs address more subtle agendas, see themselves, and are seen, as wider statements about both industries and exhibitors than the banal roll-out of new products that characterised so many fairs in the past. Today, concepts of dialogue and communication are as crucial as product presentation. Corporate presence and personality are now the keys to a successful fair appearance, and designers are becoming increasingly adept at finding the right visual and physical forms for such aspirations.

The continued success of the trade fair can also be seen in its degree of internationalisation. The selection here shows French designers working in Germany, Germans in Tokyo, the British in Detroit. If there is a preponderance of German design work here, that is, as much as anything, a reflection of Germany's strong role as a centre for trade fairs both within Europe and internationally, while the quality of American work shows how some designers have, despite local market problems, been able to improve standards. Japan and South East Asia seem still to be waiting on recovery from their recent economic problems to feed through into new stand design.

The year 2000 also shows the trade fair stand concept reinventing itself as a thematic element in a temporary exhibition. This is the thinking behind the Millennium Dome in Greenwich, London, and the EXPO 2000 in Hanover: sponsored displays that explain and entertain around a particular subject. Educational displays have been a regular feature of international exhibitions in the past, such as the Dome of Discovery at the 1951 Festival of Britain or Habitat at the Montreal Expo 67.

In making this selection for the 2000 yearbook, I have tried not only to reflect on this development, with work from both London and Hanover, but to look beyond the traditional definitions of the stand to applications that share its ethos and role. So I have included visitor centres and semi-permanent exhibits, and show trains and trucks. This is not just millennial affectation, but rather an attempt to demonstrate the role in current design practice of what could be termed "exhibit design," of which trade fair design is a major part.

Diese und ähnliche Versuche deuten darauf hin, daß die Messe weiterhin eine wichtige Rolle spielen wird. Dies bedeutet aber nicht, daß Standarchitekten Internet und World Wide Web ignorieren dürfen. Viele von ihnen sind bereits dabei, Computer in das Standdesign mit einzubeziehen, um Messebesuchern den Zugang zu Websites oder Intranets zu ermöglichen.

Die wohl bedeutendste Entwicklung ist, daß Messestände Herstellerhierarchien und nationale Klassifizierungen – das schlimmste Erbe der traditionellen Weltausstellungen – heute hinter sich gelassen haben. Die moderne Messe hat ein subtileres Programm und wird sowohl von der Industrie als auch den Ausstellern mehr als umfassende Repräsentantin betrachtet, denn als banale Darstellerin neuer Produkte. Heute sind Dialog- und Kommunikationskonzepte genauso wichtig wie Produktdarstellung. Firmenpräsenz und Persönlichkeit sind die Schlüssel zu einem erfolgreichen Messeauftritt, und Designer haben ein sicheres Gespür dafür entwickelt, dieses Ziel durch stimmige visuelle und gegenständliche Darstellungen zu erreichen.

Den fortwährenden Erfolg der Messe kann man auch am Grad ihrer Internationalisierung erkennen. Die Auswahl in diesem Buch reicht von französischen Designern, die in Deutschland arbeiten, über Deutsche in Tokio hin zu Briten in Detroit. Die große Auswahl an deutschen Designs spiegelt die starke Rolle wider, die Deutschland als Zentrum für Messen in Europa und weltweit erreicht hat. Während die Qualität amerikanischer Beispiele zeigt, daß einige Designer trotz örtlicher Marktprobleme in der Lage gewesen sind, das Niveau anzuheben, scheint man in Japan und Südostasien noch darauf zu warten, daß die wirtschaftliche Erholung von der letzten Krise auch in neue Standdesigns einfließt.

Das Jahr 2000 belebt die Idee des Messestands auch in anderer Hinsicht wieder: als thematisches Element in einer temporären Ausstellung. Dieser Gedanke steckt hinter dem Millennium Dome in Greenwich, London, und der EXPO 2000 in Hannover: Gesponserte Pavillons, die rund um ein bestimmtes Sujet erklären und unterhalten. Pädagogische Pavillons, wie der „Dome of Discovery" beim britischen Festival 1951 oder „Habitat" auf der Montreal Expo 67, sind seit jeher fester Bestandteil internationaler Ausstellungen gewesen.

For the notion of exhibit design combines two somewhat contradictory but interesting concepts. The first is the current passion with brands and the "brand experience." The commercial brand is, like the trade fair, a nineteenth century invention, and attempts to add what would not be termed associative brand values can be found in early advertising. The contemporary brand experience perhaps began in 1955 with Disneyland, the first modern theme park, and has extended across the shopping streets and malls of the world ever since. The urban visual environment has become dominated, in certain areas, by brand names, whether through advertising, signage or shopfronts. The brand experience we are endlessly invited to enjoy is intended to show that a service element is part of the corporate offer, and so represents the realignment of companies from producers of goods to providers of services. This brand exposure is a current fact of life, desirable or not, and one area in which it can be studied best is the trade fair. Many companies are realising that integrated presentation strategies are the key to brand awareness, and so linking corporate, advertising, packaging, website and stand design into a visually unified whole, particularly for major public access events.

The second concept is that the exhibit design environment is one of the few areas left for experimental architectural design. The temporary nature of the structures, the lack of any need for weatherproofing, the absence of planning controls create an immediate opportunity for exuberant expression, tempered today only by the client's brief, which will often be looking for convergence with other brand and identity elements. The classic example of this is Mies van de Rohe's 1929 Barcelona pavilion, an icon of modern architecture. And it is worth recalling that the Crystal Palace that housed the Great Exhibition was also a highly innovatory building. The continuing ability of designers to respond to such opportunities is reflected in the following pages, for example in the Journey building by Imagination and Kauffmann Theilig & Partner's Festhalle installation for Mercedes Benz.

In selecting work for inclusion I have tried to look at ways in which in this millennial year the definitions of the trade fair stand are being extended. Beyond that I have sought to focus on the two qualities of presenting the brand and designing in innovative ways.

Bei meiner Auswahl für das Jahrbuch 2000 habe ich versucht, nicht nur diese Entwicklung mit Arbeiten aus London und Hannover widerzuspiegeln, sondern über traditionelle Messestände hinaus auf ganze neue Anwendungen zu blicken. Deswegen sind Besucherzentren und dauerhafte Ausstellungen, Wanderausstellungen in Zügen und Lastwagen mit aufgenommen. Nicht aus einer Millennium-Laune heraus, sondern um zu zeigen, wie umfassend die Bedeutung von Messedesign im gesamten derzeitigen Ausstellungsdesign geworden ist.

Die Vorstellung vom Ausstellungsdesign verbindet zwei eigentlich gegensätzliche, aber interessante Elemente. Das erste beinhaltet die derzeitige Vorliebe für Marken und „Markenerlebnisse". Das Firmenzeichen ist, wie auch die Messe, eine Erfindung des 19. Jahrhunderts. Ansätze, etwas in der Werbung einzusetzen, was wir heute als Markenqualität bezeichnen würden, findet man schon früh. Die zeitgenössische Markenerfahrung fing vermutlich 1955 mit Disneyland, dem ersten modernen Vergnügungspark an, und hat sich seitdem über die Einkaufsstraßen und Einkaufszentren der Welt ausgebreitet. Das optische Umfeld der Städte wird in manchen Gegenden von Markennamen beherrscht, teils über Werbung, teils über Schilder oder Schaufenstergestaltung. Die Freude an der Markenerfahrung, zu der wir ständig eingeladen werden, soll uns zeigen, daß das Element Kundendienst Teil des Firmenangebots ist und die Umwandlung der Firma vom Warenhersteller zum Dienstleistungsbetrieb signalisiert. Das Gefühl des Ausgeliefertseins, ob man es nun mag oder nicht, ist eine harte Tatsache die nirgendwo besser zu erfahren ist, als auf einer Messe. Viele Firmen haben erkannt, daß eine abgestimmte Marketingstrategie der Schlüssel zum Markenbewußtsein ist und verbinden deshalb Werbung, Verpackung, Website, und Standarchitektur optisch zu einem einheitlichen Ganzen – besonders bei wichtigen öffentlichen Veranstaltungen.

Das zweite Element besteht in den Möglichkeiten, welche das Feld der Ausstellungen experimenteller Architektur noch läßt. Die Tatsache, daß die Bauten nur für kurze Dauer bestehen, nicht wetterfest sein müssen und keinen Kontrollen unterliegen, schaffen den Nährboden für überschwengliche Ausdrucksformen, die nur durch die Anweisungen des Kunden, der sich oft an anderen Marken orientiert, im Zaum gehalten werden. Das klassische Beispiel ist Mies van de Rohes Barcelona Pavillon (1929), eine Ikone moderner Architektur.

As I believe that quality shows through in depth, I have not hesitated to include more than one project from several of the design teams chosen. What has most impressed me is the maturity of the visual language used by many of the designers, their mastery of colour, drama and effect, and their ability to find effective visual metaphors for the complex offers their clients wish to convey. These factors seem to me to underpin the continuing role of the trade fair as a method of corporate communication.

Does this mean that there are no problems facing the future of trade fairs and their design? Not quite. One thing that is holding back the development of better design in the USA, for example, is the practice of free pitching, whereby designers offer a preliminary design idea to a client without charge in the hope of getting the full job. This is not in the long-term interests of the client or the designer, and only in the short-term interests of the client, who gets a few rushed ideas for nothing. Costs are pushing some smaller fairs to the edge, while the big fairs just get bigger. But there is, I suspect, a limit to the feasible size of a fair, both upper and lower. Fair organisers and stand designers, and their clients, will have to balance these factors, as well as looking continuously at the opportunities offered for corporate communication by other media, including the Internet and Web. By learning from these other disciplines, stand design can only improve and meet the challenges of the new century.

Auch der Kristall Palast, Heimat der Weltausstellung, war ein außergewöhnlich innovatives Gebäude. Die unverminderte Fähigkeit von Designern, auf solche Chancen zu reagieren spiegelt sich in den folgenden Seiten wider, z.B. im Pavillon „Journey" von Imagination und im Mercedes-Benz Auftritt von Kauffmann Theilig & Partner.

Bei der Auswahl für dieses Buch habe ich versucht aufzuzeigen, wie in diesem Millennium-Jahr die Definition des Messestands erweitert wird. Außerdem habe ich mich auf die zwei Qualitätsmerkmale Markenpräsentation und Innovation konzentriert. Da ich daran glaube, daß sich innere Qualität durchsetzt, habe ich nicht gezögert, von einigen der Designteams mehrere Projekte auszuwählen. Was mich am meisten beeindruckt hat, ist die Reife der visuellen Ausdrucksweise vieler Designer, ihr meisterhafter Umgang mit Farbe, Drama und Effekt und ihr Talent, optische Metaphern für die komplexen Angebote zu finden, die ihre Kunden vermitteln wollen. Diese Faktoren scheinen mir die anhaltende Bedeutung der Messe als Mittel zur Kommunikation unter Firmen zu bestätigen.

Bedeutet das, daß die Zukunft keine Probleme für Messen und deren Gestaltung bereithält? Nicht ganz. Ein Grund für die stagnierende Entwicklung von gutem Design in den USA ist z.B. die Praxis des „free pitching", bei dem Designer den potentiellen Kunden einen ersten Entwurf vorstellen, ohne eine Rechnung zu stellen, in der Hoffnung den Auftrag zu erhalten. Auf Dauer ist das weder im Interesse des Kunden noch des Designers und nur kurzfristig von Reiz für den Kunden, der umsonst einen eilig ausgeführten Entwurf erhält. Während Investitionskosten einige der kleinen Messen an den Rand der Existenz treiben, werden große Messen immer größer. Ich glaube aber, daß es eine Ober- sowie eine Untergrenze gibt, was die Größe von Messen betrifft. Messeveranstalter, Standarchitekten und deren Kunden werden diese Faktoren ausbalancieren müssen und ständig ein Auge auf andere Möglichkeiten der Firmenkommunikation wie Internet und World Wide Web behalten müssen. Wenn man von diesen Medien lernt, kann Messestanddesign nur besser und den Anforderungen des neuen Jahrhunderts gerecht werden.

Conway Lloyd Morgan, London, March 2000

Conway Lloyd Morgan, London, März 2000

Millennial Moments

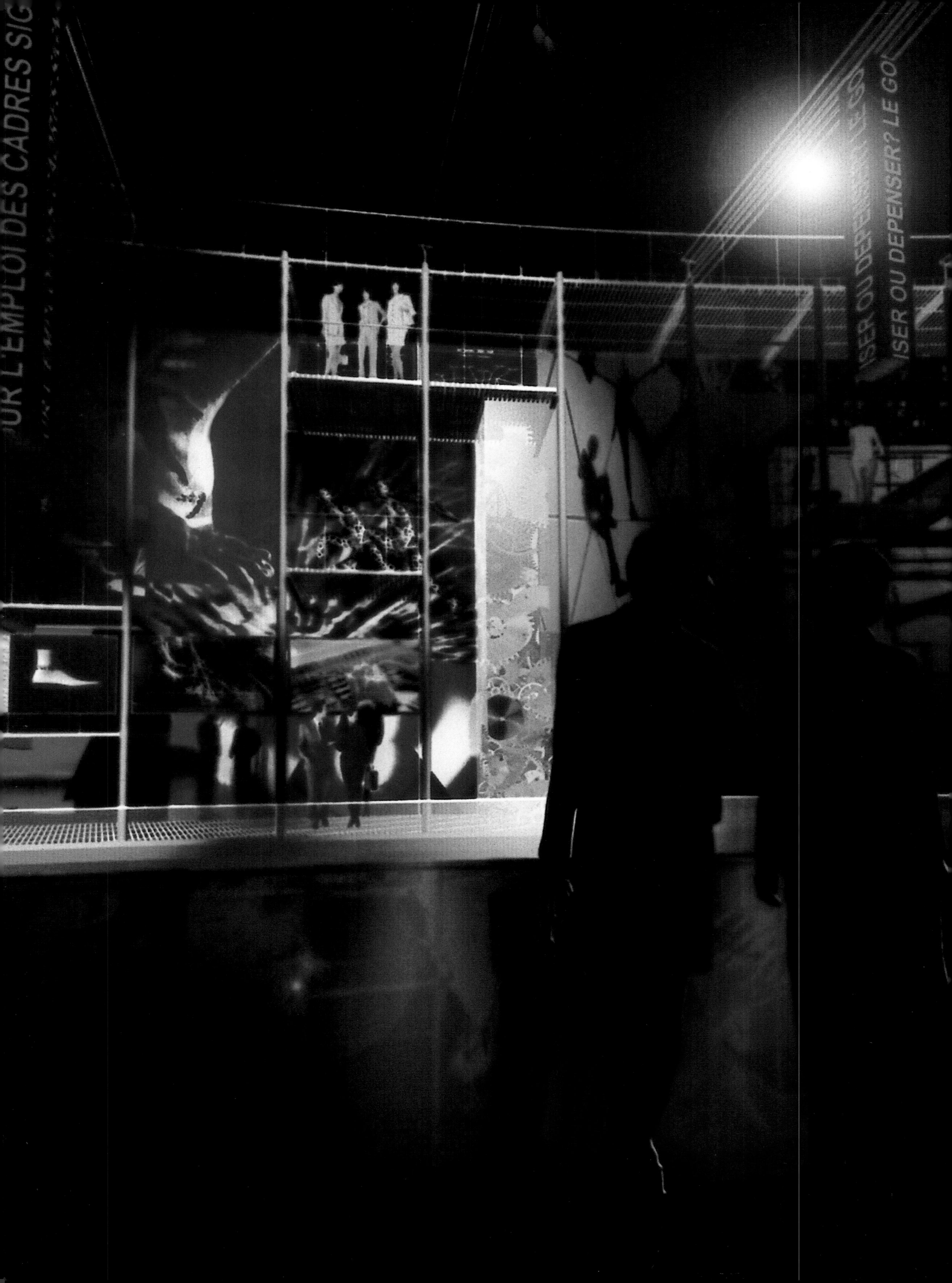
UR L'EMPLOI DES CADRES SIG
ISER OU DEPENSER? LE GO

Commodity, firmness and delight

Kommerz und Vergnügen

Jean Nouvel for
Hanover's EXPO

Jean Nouvel für die
EXPO Hannover

"I propose the accessibility of the real through the virtual, through the image behind the image." So Jean Nouvel describes his approach to his two projects at EXPO 2000 in Hanover. Such an event, he suggests, "should astonish the conscience of the visitor through its evaluation of the world, in relation to the notions of modernity, emergence and the future." So while his projects about Mobility and The Future of Work deal with current problems and possible solutions, their overall vision is far broader.

„Ich schlage den Zugang zur Realität durch das Virtuelle, durch das Bildnis hinter dem Bildnis vor." So beschreibt Jean Nouvel den Ansatz zu seinen beiden Projekten auf der EXPO 2000 in Hannover. Seiner Meinung nach „sollte dieses Ereignis das Bewußtsein des Besuchers erstaunen und seine Vorstellungen von Modernität, Aufbruch und Zukunft in Beziehung setzen zu seiner Wahrnehmung der gesamten Welt." Deshalb ist auch die Palette seiner Projekte über Mobilität und die Zukunft der Arbeit breiter angelegt, als nur aktuelle Probleme und Lösungsmöglichkeiten aufzuzeigen.

Above: Computer visualisation showing the scale of
the torus ramp

Following page: The interface between the torus and
the main Mobility display

Oben: Computer-Visuali-
sierung, die die Größe der
kreisförmigen Rampe zeigt

Nächste Seite: Verbindung
zwischen der Rampe und
der Haupt-Ausstellung

Detail of the wall panels
from the Mobility exhibit

Wanddetails innerhalb der
Mobilitäts-Ausstellung

For the concepts of mobility (especially personal mobility) and motion (from the sub-atomic level to the galactic plane), as Nouvel points out, are among the central mythologies of the 20th century, whether through objects such as cars, boats and planes, or metaphors such as personal trajectories, response speeds, chaos theory. Nouvel offers the visitor a physical and visual journey through a series of immense images contrasting and comparing the actual and the potential of the subject, at different scales and speeds, contradictory and complex. Holographs transport the viewer both within and outside objects, repetitive motifs of the known dissolve into enduring fragments of potential.

Die Vorstellungen von Mobilität (besonders persönlicher Mobilität) und Bewegung (vom sub-atomaren Niveau bis zu galaktischen Ebenen) sind, wie Nouvel andeutet, Teil des zentralen Mythos des 20. Jahrhunderts, symbolisiert durch Objekte wie Auto, Schiff und Flugzeug oder durch Metaphern wie „persönliche Flugbahnen", Reaktionsgeschwindigkeit, Chaos-Theorie. Nouvel bietet dem Besucher anhand einer Reihe von großartigen Abbildungen in verschiedenen Dimensionen und Tempi eine körperliche und visuelle Reise, die das Tatsächliche mit dem Potential, welches dieses Thema beinhaltet, konfrontieren und vergleichen. Holographien führen den Betrachter in Objekte und wieder hinaus, wiederholte Motive verschmelzen in dauerhafte Teile des Möglichen.

Visualisation of the Mobility
display main corridor

Visualisierung des Haupt-
Ausstellungs-Korridors
„Mobilität"

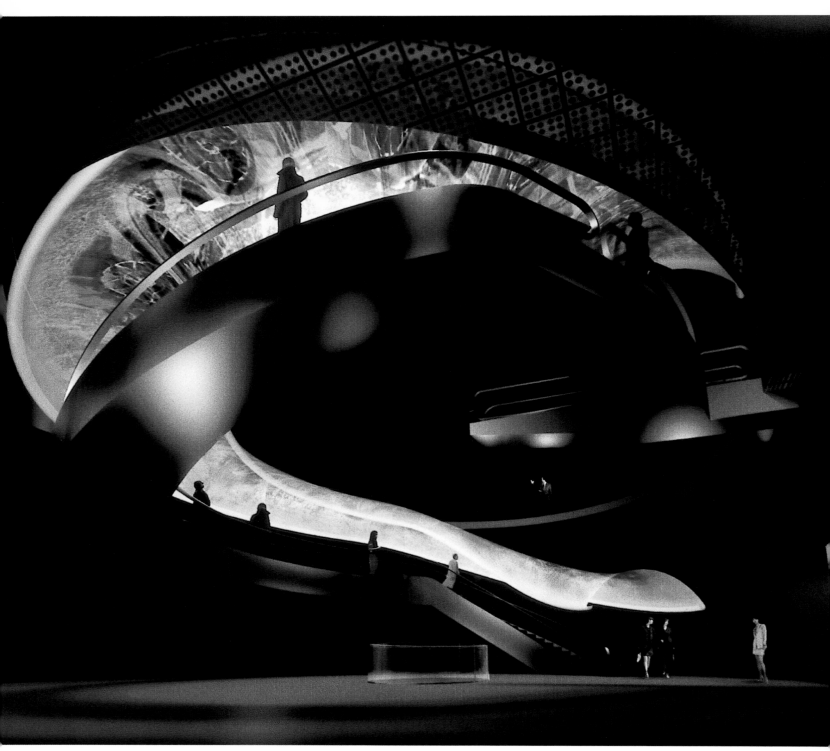

The entrance to Mobility is via a torus ramp leading down into the main display corridor. The fluidity of the shape is in itself a statement about mobility.

Der Eintritt zur „Mobiltität" führt über eine kreisförmige Rampe hinunter in den Haupt-Ausstellungs-Korridor. Die fließenden Formen verbildlichen Mobilität.

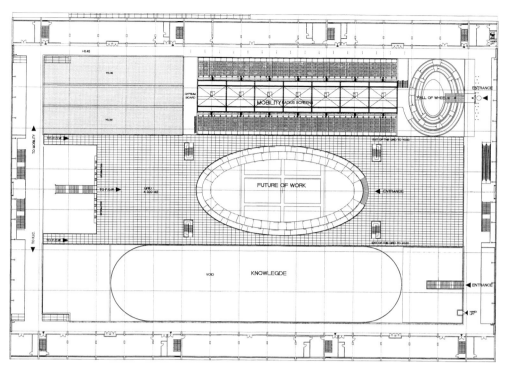

Plan of the two exhibition
areas designed by Nouvel
at EXPO 2000

Grundriß der zwei Ausstel-
lungsbereiche, entworfen
von Nouvel für die EXPO
2000

Year	**2000**
Location	**Hanover**
Pavilion	**Mobility**
Exhibitor	**EXPO 2000**
Concept	**Architectures Jean Nouvel, Paris**
Design team	**Jean Nouvel, Hubert Tonka, Hala Wardé, Elisabeth Kather, Sandro Carbone, Pascaline Paris, Anne Lamiable, Jane Landrey Employees: Elke Seipp, Peter Kiess**
Lighting	**Roberto Venturi**
Multi-media team	**Mounir El Hawat (AJN) Michel Cova (DUCKS)**
Graphics	**Cédric Niesser, Marie Maillard (Artefactory)**
Size	**3,500 m²**
Photos	**Artefactory**

A series of scenarios, involving photographic and digital images, human actors and robots, spell out the reality and potential of the workplace in original and different ways.

Eine Serie von Szenarien:
Fotografien und digitale Bilder, menschliche Akteure und Roboter. Gezeigt wird die Realität und das Potential des Arbeitsplatzes in ursprünglicher und abgewandelter Form.

Work is another myth of modern times. To put it into context, Nouvel reverses the ideas of a theatre, with the audience on stage and the actors around them, and a series of questions suspended above. From a totality of different scenarios the visitor has the opportunity of reflection and choice. Work is presented as a mute human condition, in which the accessories have as much symbolic value as the actors. This process of engagement avoids the banalities of statistics and status quo analysis that so often surround the question of work.

Nouvel's commitment to the modern, his understanding of the ambiguities of solidity and light, his intellectual and analytical approach single him out among his contemporaries. His proposals for Hanover embody a profound understanding of the complexities of the present linked to an architectonic mise en scene, a vehicle for exploring the imagination of the future and the mythology of the actual. As he himself says "the image is the key but also the question. This is a metaphysical situation. Emerging permanance in which the mobility of the future is faced by what is eternal."

Auch Arbeit ist ein Mythos unserer Zeit. Um die Zusammenhänge darzustellen, dreht Nouvel die Grundidee des Theaters um: Die Zuschauer sind auf der Bühne, die Schauspieler in den Rängen, und über dem Ganzen hängt eine Serie von Fragen. In unterschiedlichen Szenarien hat der Besucher die Möglichkeit zur Reflexion und Auswahl. Arbeit wird als ein sprachloser menschlicher Zustand dargestellt, in dem die gewissen Extras genauso viel symbolische Bedeutung haben wie die Darsteller. Diese Form der Auseinandersetzung umgeht die Banalität von Statistiken und Status-Quo-Analysen, welche so oft Fragen zur Arbeit begleiten.

Nouvels Hingabe zur Moderne, sein Verständnis von Zweideutigkeit von Stabilität und Licht, seine intellektuelle und analytische Annäherung machen ihn einzigartig unter seinen Zeitgenossen. Seine Vorschläge für Hannover zeigen ein tiefes Verständnis für die Komplexitäten der Gegenwart, verbunden mit einem architektonischen „in Szene setzen", einem Mittel, um die Vorstellungen der Zukunft und die Mythologie des Heute zu ergründen. Er selber behauptet: „Das Bild ist der Schlüssel und gleichzeitig die Frage". Dies ist eine metaphysische Situation. So entsteht Beständigkeit, in der die Beweglichkeit der Zukunft mit dem Ewigen konfrontiert wird.

Images from the scenarios
for the Future of Work

Szenarien für die Zukunft
der Arbeit

Year	**2000**
Location	**Hanover**
Pavilion	**Future of Work**
Exhibitor	**EXPO 2000**
Concept	**Architectures Jean Nouvel, Paris**
Design team	**Jean Nouvel, Hubert Tonka, Hala Wardé, Julie Parmentier, Sandro Carbone, Stacy Eisenberg, Pascaline Paris, Anne Lamiable**
Lighting	**Roberto Venturi**
Multi-media team	**Mounir El Hawat (AJN) Michel Cova (DUCKS)**
Graphics	**Marie Maillard, Cendrine Bonamy**
Size	**3,500 m²**
Photos	**Artefactory**

Talking Travels
Sprach-Reisen

Imagination for the
Millennium Dome

Imagination für den
Millennium Dome

The Millennium Dome in London is, together with Hanover's EXPO 2000, one of the largest celebrations of the beginning of the 21st century and the new millennium in the world. (In this context, it is worth recalling that the original concept for the Dome was a joint proposal by Richard Rogers and Partners, the architects, and Imagination, the London design and communication company with a strong reputation in trade fair and event design. And there are those who regret that the project was finally developed by others.) Within the 100,000 square metres area of the Dome are fourteen special pavilions, a central show area, restaurants and bars and merchandising areas.

Der Millennium Dome in London ist, zusammen mit der EXPO 2000 in Hannover, eine der größten Veranstaltungen anläßlich des 21. Jahrhunderts und des neuen Millenniums. (In diesem Zusammenhang darf man nicht vergessen, daß das Originalkonzept für den Dom ein gemeinsames Projekt der Architekten Richard Rogers & Partner und Imagination war, einer etablierten Londoner Design- und Kommunikationsfirma im Bereich Messe- und Event-Design. Und es gibt Stimmen des Bedauerns darüber, daß das Projekt letztendlich von anderen weiterentwickelt wurde.) Innerhalb der 100.000 m² Grundfläche des Doms gibt es 14 individuelle Pavillons, eine zentrale Ausstellungsfläche, Restaurants, Bars und eine Verkaufsfläche.

Above: In the Talk zone
messages created by visi-
tors are projected around
the interior and on exterior
panels.

Right: Part of the gallery
demonstrating the role of
conversation and talk in
communication.

Oben: In der „Talk-Zone"
werden von Besuchern ver-
faßte Botschaften auf die
inneren und äußeren Schei-
ben projiziert.

Rechts: Teil der Galerie, der
die Bedeutung von Konver-
sation und Reden demon-
striert.

It is a festival, a showcase, a classroom and a celebration, borrowings its idioms from the circus, the boardwalk, the didactic exhibition and the trade fair. Within this medley Imagination has created two very different "zones", Journey, sponsored by Ford of Europe, and Talk, sponsored by BT.

The "two" zones are visually distinct: Talk is a pair of buildings, leaning slightly together like two talking heads, white and translucent. The visitor follows a two level pathway through and between these, being offered explanations, information and concepts centred on the key role of verbal communication in the contemporary world. Towards the end of the tour the visitors have the opportunity to talk themselves: by creating a message to be written out on the luminous pathways on the exterior, by creating an avatar for a website, by sending an email message. The key to this is density and multiplicity (such as one finds in conversation) and it is achieved here through the torrent of images, video or still, and the layering of texts and information on wall surfaces and overlaid transparent panels. The whole moves from explanation to extrapolation, providing an understanding of the role of communication in the next century, with an opportunity to try out in an involving way some of its possibilities. This follows a path from darker to lighter spaces – a literal enlightenment.

Es ist ein Festspiel, ein Schaufenster, ein Klassenzimmer, eine Feier, mit Redewendungen geborgt von Zirkus, Strandpromenade, didaktischer Ausstellung und Messe. Innerhalb dieser Mischung hat Imagination zwei sehr unterschiedliche „Zonen" erschaffen, „Journey", gesponsert von Ford Europa und „Talk", gesponsert von BT (British Telecommunications).

Diese zwei „Zonen" weichen optisch sehr voneinander ab: „Talk" besteht aus zwei Bauten, weiß und durchsichtig, die sich einander – wie Gesprächspartner – leicht zubeugen. Der Besucher folgt einem Pfad, der auf zwei Ebenen durch die Gebäude und zwischen ihnen hindurch führt. Er erhält dabei Erläuterungen und Informationen zur Schlüsselrolle der verbalen Kommunikation in der heutigen Welt. Gegen Ende der Tour haben die Besucher die Gelegenheit, selbst zu sprechen: Indem sie eine Nachricht hinterlassen, die auf den beleuchteten Pfaden an der Außenwand erscheint, oder indem sie einen Avatar für eine Website erstellen oder eine E-Mail verschicken. Die Grundidee des Stands besteht in Dichte und Vielfalt (wie in einem Gespräch) und wird erreicht durch eine Flut von Abbildungen, Videos oder Stills sowie die Schichtung von Text und Information auf Wänden und überlagerten Transparenttafeln. Das Ganze bewegt sich von Erklärung zu Extrapolation und vermittelt dadurch Verständnis für die Rolle der Kommunikation im 21. Jahrhundert bis hin zur aktiven Erfahrung: man folgt einem Pfad von dunklen zu helleren Räumen – einer buchstäblichen Erleuchtung.

Above: The bridge linking
the two buildings of the
Talk zone

Right: Details showing the
relation between interior
and exterior spaces

Oben: Die Brücke: Verbin-
dungsstück für die zwei
Gebäude der „Talk-Zone"

Rechts: Details der inneren
und äußeren Räume

Year	**2000**
Location	**Greenwich, Great Britain**
Trade Fair	**Millennium Dome Talk Zone**
Exhibitor	**British Telecommunications plc**
Concept	**Imagination Ltd., London**
Design team	**Lana Duroivic, Jo Sampson, Catherine Willis, Jason Bruges, Rupert Bassett, Kelvin Smith, Andy Holt**
Lighting	**Steve Latham, Mike Sobotniki, Neil Austin, Patrick Murray (Imagination)**
Realisation	**Scena**
Size	**1,500 m²**
Photos	**Imagination Ltd.**

The Journey building, whose iconic arms are visible above the auditorium area of the whole Dome, is denser and more complex still. The visitor swerves through a series of presentations at the start, rich in visual and acoustic content, swirling in black and red, telling in detail and (no pun) at speed the history of transport and its role in human society. One moment the visitor is looking at Blériot's monoplane, the next at the Bullet Train, a Chinese junk or Malcolm Campbell's Bluebird speed record car. At the moment of overload, both for the visitor and the planet, it seems, a moment of cool white reflection, before passing into a display of concept vehicles, from space vehicles to undersea crawlers to single seat racers. Some of these designs represent commercial projects, others are student visualisations. Together they offer a range of options for thinking about the future of travel. From them the visitor passes into a grey and yellow area, with the opportunity to reply to the issues raised by the preceding sections. The colour transitions set a mood and guide the viewer, through information, possibilities and response, making the visitor feel involved with the project and its ambitions.

The two stands, in their different ways, meet the ideal condition of the Dome, to balance entertainment and information, presence and futurability, visuals and vision. They do so with a dexterity and sophistication, and with an attention to design detail and depth of content that is exemplary.

Der „Journey"-Pavillon, dessen ikonenhafte Arme über die Auditoriumsfläche des gesamten Doms hinaus sichtbar sind, ist noch dichter und komplexer. Der Besucher „biegt" am Anfang in eine Reihe von Bildern ein, die reich an optischem und akustischem Inhalt sind, in schwarz und rot wirbeln und rasant die Geschichte der Beförderung sowie ihre Rolle in der Gesellschaft darstellen. Im ersten Moment sieht der Besucher Blériots Eindecker, im nächsten den Bullett Train, dann eine chinesische Dschunke oder Malcolm Campbells Rekordauto Bluebird. Im Augenblick der Überladung – bezogen sowohl auf die Bilder als auch den Planeten – , gibt es einen Moment der kühl-weißen Besinnlichkeit, dann geht es weiter in eine Ausstellung von Konzeptfahrzeugen, Weltraumfahrzeugen, Unterwassercrawlern, Einsitzerrennwagen. Einige der Entwürfe sind kommerzielle Projekte, andere basieren auf Ideen von Studenten. Zusammen bieten sie zukünftige Möglichkeiten, das Reisen neu zu überdenken. Die Besucher gehen zuletzt in einen grau-gelben Bereich, in dem sie die Möglichkeit haben, Antworten auf die vorher gestellten Fragen zu finden. Der Farbwechsel bewirkt eine neue Stimmung und führt den Betrachter durch Information und Interaktion.

Die zwei Stände erfüllen auf unterschiedliche Weise die gebotenen Voraussetzungen des Doms, Unterhaltung und Information, Gegenwart und Zukunft, Sichtbares und Seherisches auszubalancieren. Dies tun sie mit Gewandtheit und Raffinesse, mit Liebe zum Detail und einer inhaltlichen Tiefe, die beispielhaft ist.

A replica of Blériot's mono-plane (left) dominates the first part of the Journey zone, leading to a "quiet space" (right) for reflection.

Eine Nachbau von Blériots Eindecker (links) dominiert den vorderen Teil der „Journey Zone" und führt zu einem ruhigen „Besinnungs-Raum" (rechts).

The gallery of new concepts in travel (above), from airships to submersibles, leads to a series of opportunities to address and vote on specific questions about the future (right).

Die Galerie mit neuen Mobilitätskonzepten (oben), mit Luftschiffen und tauchfähigen Objekten, ermöglicht die Reflexion und Bewertung zukünftiger Fragen (rechts).

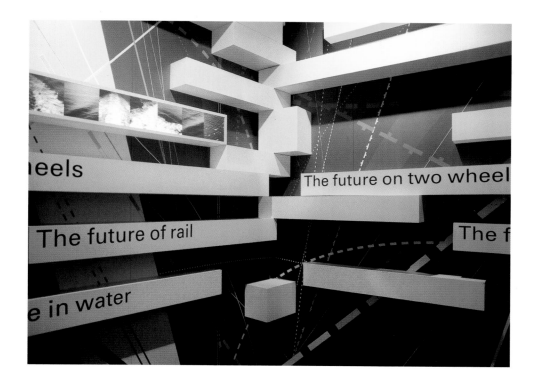

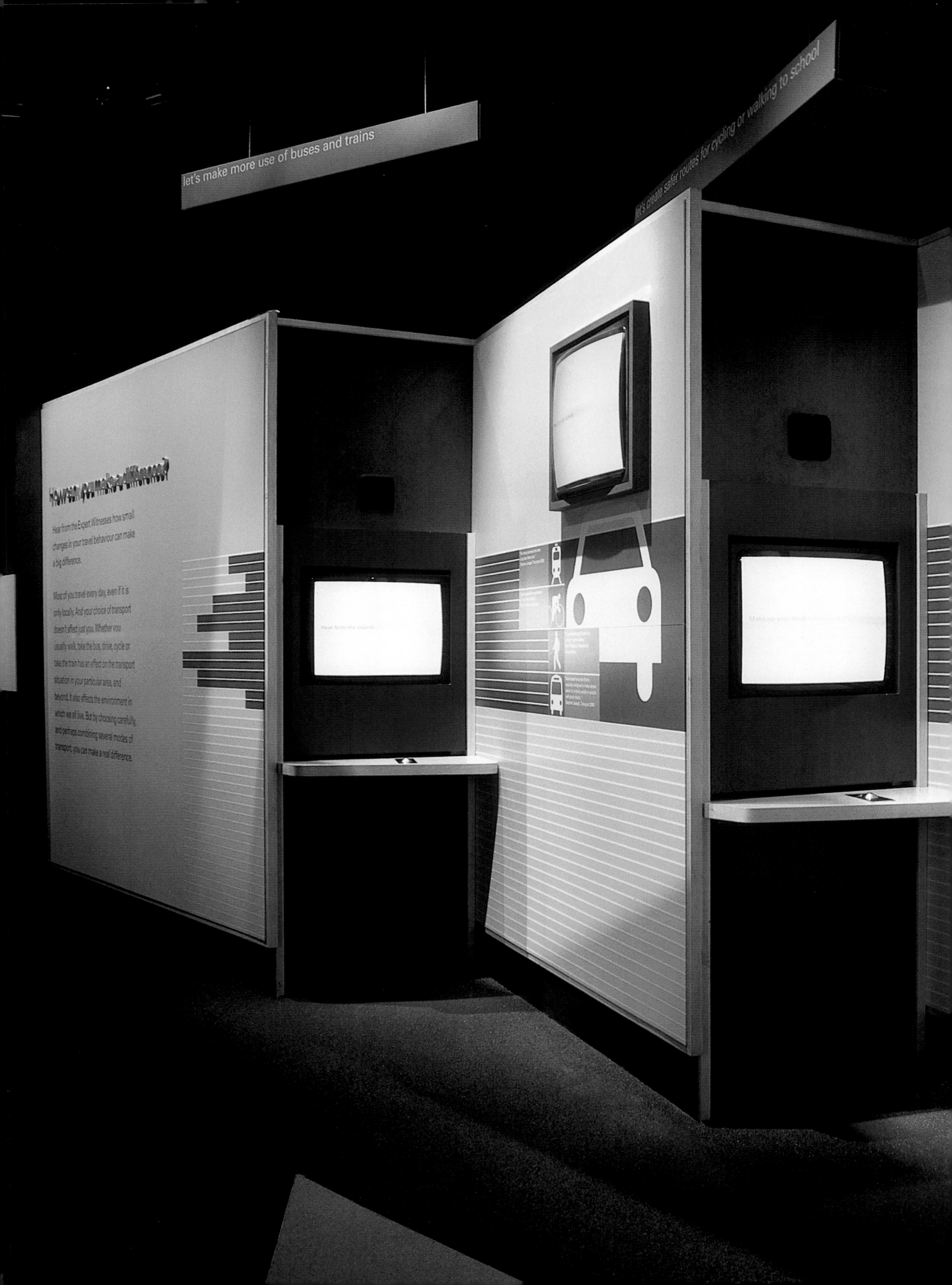

How can you make a difference?

Hear from the Expert Witnesses how small changes in your travel behaviour can make a big difference.

Most of you travel every day, even if it is only locally. And your choice of transport doesn't affect just you. Whether you usually walk, take the bus, drive, cycle or take the train has an effect on the transport situation in your particular area, and beyond. It also affects the environment in which we all live. But by choosing carefully, and perhaps combining several modes of transport, you can make a real difference.

Hear from the experts

Make up your mind

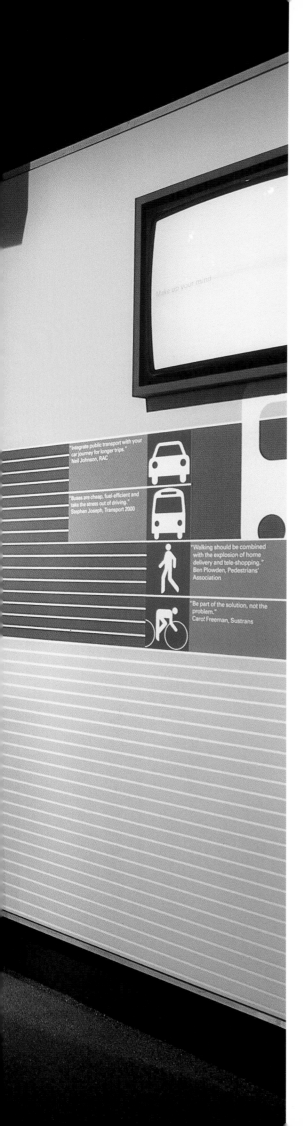

Year	**2000**
Location	**Greenwich, Great Britain**
Trade Fair	**Millennium Dome Journey Zone**
Exhibitor	**Ford Motor Company**
Concept	**Imagination Ltd., London**
Design team	**Alistair Petrie, Scott Theobold, Rob Hearne, Derek Shears, Martin Brown**
Lighting	**Steve Latham, Mike Sobotniki, Patrick Murray (Imagination)**
Multi-media team	**Martin Codd, Ben Hughes (Imagination)**
Realisation	**Britlands, KP Martin**
Size	**2,100 m²**
Photos	**Imagination Ltd., London**

Take the A-Train

Oliver Schrott Kommunikation
for Opel

Oliver Schrott Kommunikation
für Opel

An unusual brief: a stand 280 metres long, but under 2 metres wide, and able to go round corners. That was the requirement for the Opel Millennium Express, which toured the rail networks of continental Europe in 1999 and 2000. Designed by Oliver Schrott Kommunikation, the train celebrated both 100 years of Opel's history and its vision of the future of transport.

The 'stand' consisted of 42 purpose built containers mounted on 14 wagons. While this means a narrow site, the team managed to incorporate five special glass containers to display historic cars, new models and concept vehicles. Information terminals, DVD players and other multimedia features (including a holographic projection and a 360 degree cinema) completed the display.

Ein ungewöhnlicher Auftrag: ein 280 m langer, aber weniger als 2 m breiter Messestand, der sich um Ecken winden kann. Das waren die Vorgaben für den Opel Millennium Express, der 1999 und 2000 durch Europa fuhr. Der Zug, ein Entwurf von Oliver Schrott Kommunikation, zelebrierte sowohl 100 Jahre Opel Geschichte als auch Opels Vision vom Transport der Zukunft.

Der „Stand" umfaßte 42, nur für diesen Zweck gebaute Container, welche auf 14 Waggons montiert waren. Trotz der schmalen Grundfläche waren fünf spezielle Glas-Container miteingebaut, in denen historische Autos, neue Modelle und Konzeptfahrzeuge ausgestellt werden konnten. Informationsstationen, DVD-Spieler und andere Multimedia-Installationen (einschließlich einer holographischen Projektion und einem Eyemax Kino) vervollständigten die Ausstellung.

The outside of the train also provided over 1,000 square meters for displays of photographic imagery.

The exhibits looked at the history of Opel, its currents models and policies (including sports sponsorship) as well as wider issues such as transport policy integration, new fuels and safety systems. The choice of a train as display unit emphasises these aspects, as well as allowing the exhibit to visit over a dozen European countries.

Die Außenwände mit über 1.000 Quadratmetern wurden als Darstellungsfläche für fotografische Abbildungen genutzt.

Die Ausstellungsstücke beleuchteten die Geschichte von Opel und präsentierten aktuelle Modelle, die Produktpolitik (einschließlich der Sportförderung), sowie Aussagen zu verkehrspolitischer Integration, neuen Treibstoffen und Sicherheitssystemen. Die Entscheidung, einen Zug als Ausstellungsfläche zu verwenden, betonte diese Aspekte. Gleichzeitig war es dadurch möglich, mit der Ausstellung mehr als ein Dutzend europäischer Länder zu besuchen.

Container F   Container D   Container G

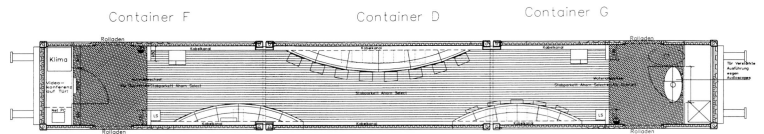

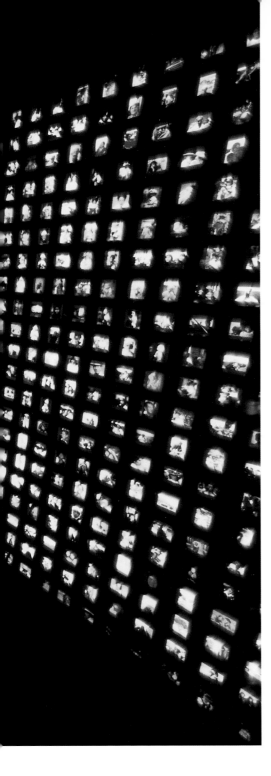

Year	**1999/2000**
Location	**1999 - Germany, Spain, Portugal, Belgium, France, Italy; 2000 - Hungary, Croatia, Austria, Slowenia, Switzerland, The Czech Republic**
Trade Fair	**Opel Millenium Express, Railshow in 12 countries**
Exhibitor	**GM Europe, Zurich/Adam Opel AG, Rüsselsheim**
Concept	**Oliver Schrott Kommunikation GmbH, Cologne: Achim Scheffler - Architect, Oliver Schrott - Creative Director, Guido Lenssen - Art Director**
Multi-media design	**Oliver Schrott Kommunikation GmbH**
Video design	**Mecom GmbH, Fulda / Oliver Schrott Kommunikation GmbH**
Music design	**Sonic System, Cologne: Heiner d'Alquen**
Realisation	**Ambrosius Messebau, Frankfurt am Main**
Size	**Total floor area 557 m² Exhibition area 400 m²**
Photos	**Walter Tillmann avcommunication GmbH: Frank Erber**

44

Seeds of Hope

Keime der Hoffnung

Thinc Design
for Monsanto

Thinc Design
für Monsanto

Attitudes towards genetically modified foods are a litmus test of people's attitude towards modern science. Inevitable and desirable progress, on the one hand, or interfering with nature on the other. Between the extremes, arguments of principle and detail abound. Agribusiness giant Monsanto is one of the firms caught up in the debate, since their genetically-modified seeds have a leading place on the market.

The invitation to Thinc Design to create a special Monsanto exhibit at the Epcot Centre in Florida, to stand for three years, was therefore an interesting challenge. What Tom Hennes and his colleagues realised was that the variety and diversity of nature was the key to understanding the issues.

Die Einstellung der Gesellschaft zu genetisch veränderten Lebensmitteln ist eine Art Lackmus-Test für die Einstellung zur modernen Wissenschaft: unvermeidbarer und erwünschter Fortschritt einerseits oder ein Vergehen an der Natur andererseits? Argumente zu beiden Positionen gibt es reichlich. Auch die Firma Monsanto – ein Gigant der Landwirtschaft – muß sich mit dieser Frage auseinandersetzen, da ihre genetisch veränderten Samen auf dem Markt eine Spitzenposition innehaben.

Die Einladung an Thinc Design, eine spezielle, drei Jahre dauernde Monsanto-Ausstellung für das Epcot Center in Florida zu entwerfen, war daher eine interessante Herausforderung. Tom Hennes und seinen Kollegen war bald klar, daß Vielfalt und Unterschiede in der Natur der Schlüssel zum Verständnis der Streitfrage sind.

As Hennes puts it, the exhibit is about "the beauty of understanding how to look for hidden possibilities in hidden places, the beauty of learning to look in some of the smallest places for some of the biggest possibilities. Possibilities such as curing more illnesses, growing more food and living healthier lives in a healthier environment."

The exhibit is designed to look as close to a natural environment as possible, and contains several real natural environments such as ponds and insect colonies. It is family entertainment, not corporate hard sell, with a tunnel for kids to explore, three "Look Closer Machines" and even a resident storyteller. "It's amazing what you can find when you look closer," as Hennes says.

Hennes meint, in der Ausstellung gehe es darum, „das Wunder zu verstehen, wie man an versteckten Stellen nach versteckten Möglichkeiten suchen kann, und wie man noch in kleinsten Winkeln die größten Möglichkeiten findet. Die Möglichkeit zum Beispiel, mehr Krankheiten zu heilen, mehr Nahrungsmittel anzupflanzen und ein gesünderes Leben in einer gesünderen Umwelt zu führen."

Der Entwurf der Ausstellung versucht, ein natürliches Umfeld nachzuempfinden und schließt mehrere „echte" Naturelemente wie Teiche oder Insektenkolonien ein. Mit einem Erkundungstunnel für Kinder, drei „Schau genau hin"-Maschinen und sogar einem eigenen Märchenerzähler soll die Ausstellung mehr der Familienunterhaltung als harter Verkaufspolitik dienen. „Es ist erstaunlich, was man findet, wenn man genau hinschaut", sagt Hennes.

Letting the visitors explore
the exhibit for themselves
both involves them in
Monsanto's vision and
explains the theme of
research.

Wenn die Besucher die
Ausstellung selbst erkun-
den, erhalten sie zweierlei:
Einblick in Monsantos
Visionen und Erklärungen
zum Thema Forschung.

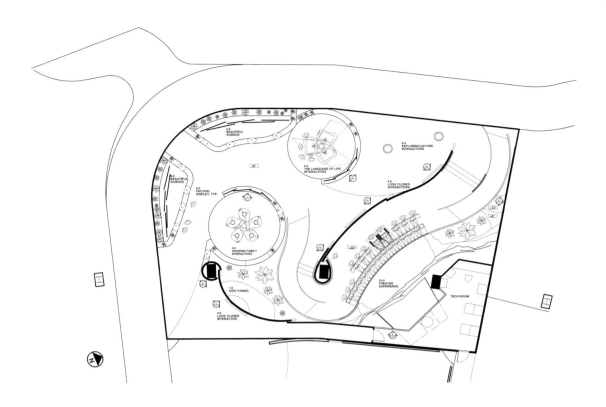

Year	**1999-2002**
Location	**Epcot, Walt Disney World, Florida**
Trade Fair	**Innoventions long-term exhibit space**
Exhibitor	**Monsanto Company**
Concept	**Thinc Design, New York**
Design team	**Tom Hennes, Jim Goldschmidt,** **Karen Gettinger, Jennifer Whitburn,** **Rick Stockton, Mario Gimpaglia**
Graphics	**Drive Communications**
Lighting	**Paul Palazzo**
Multi-media Team	**Bob Haroutunian (presentation planning),** **IXL, Zero Gravity, Bright Pictures,** **Creative Realities**
Realisation	**Cinnabar**
Size	**3,500 m² (multi-level)**
Photos	**Maureen Worrall, Jim Goldschmidt,** **Tom Hennes**

Above: Plan of the three-year exhibit

Right: A "Look Closer Machine" for exploring plant life

Oben: Grundriß der Drei-Jahres-Ausstellung

Rechts: Ein „Schau genau hin"-Modell

Black on Black

Schwarz auf Schwarz

McMillan Group for ICI

McMillan Group für ICI

ICI Americas Inc's main business is in making plastic component parts for automobiles, essential but invisible elements. So in designing a permanent exhibit for their US head quarters, McMillan Design decided to concentrate on the role of the objects, rather than their form. As Charlie McMillan explains "we blew up black and white photos of cars to huge proportions, converted these to mezzotints and silk screened these images onto glossy black glass panels, giving a matte black on gloss black image. Onto these black on black images we created large free flowing swashes of intense color against which the dark parts would contrast."

Das Kerngeschäft von ICI Americas Incorporations ist die Herstellung von Plastikteilen für Autos – wichtige, aber unsichtbare Bestandteile. Deshalb beschloß McMillan Design, sich beim Entwurf für die Dauerausstellung im amerikanischen Hauptsitz der Firma auf die Rolle des Objekts zu konzentrieren, statt auf dessen Form. Charlie McMillan erklärt: „Wir haben Schwarzweiß-Fotos von Autos gigantisch vergrößert, davon Mezzotints herstellen lassen, die wir dann per Siebdruck auf glänzend schwarze Glasplatten drucken ließen. Dadurch entstand ein matt und glänzend schwarzes Bild. Auf diese Bilder haben wir großflächig frei-fließende Formen in sehr intensiven Farben aufgetragen, um einen Kontrast mit den dunklen Stellen herzustellen."

ICI General Products

From chemicals used in the manufacture of cars to engineering plastics and products for auto safety the General Products group helps in perfecting today's concepts and delivers automotive reality.

'Emkarox'

Winnofil

ARCTON

'DIAKON'

DIAKON

KLONE

SAFFIL
Alumina Fiber

SAFFIL
SAFFIL
SAFFIL
ALUMINA FIBRES

LOW DENSITY MAT

Halon 1211

ICI Aerospace

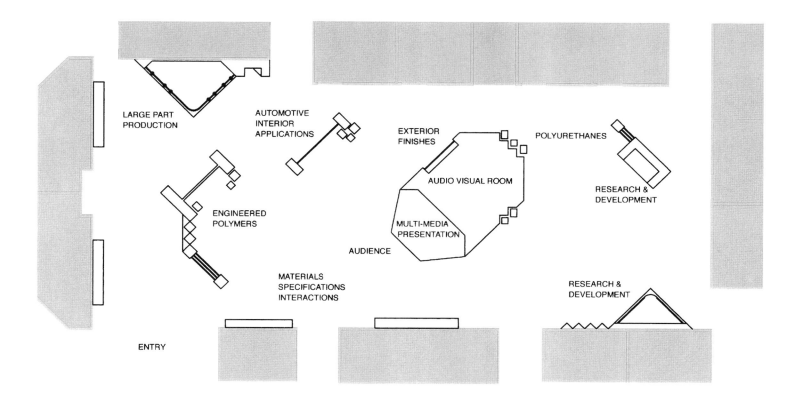

LARGE PART
PRODUCTION

AUTOMOTIVE
INTERIOR
APPLICATIONS

EXTERIOR
FINISHES

POLYURETHANES

AUDIO VISUAL ROOM

RESEARCH &
DEVELOPMENT

ENGINEERED
POLYMERS

MULTI-MEDIA
PRESENTATION

AUDIENCE

MATERIALS
SPECIFICATIONS
INTERACTIONS

RESEARCH &
DEVELOPMENT

ENTRY

ICI Americas has thirteen different manufacturing divisions, and the exhibit was intended to bring them all together, each with its own display. These displays were complemented by a specially commissioned multi-media display including film of an ICI sponsored racing car. The whole ensemble presents an overview of the company's activities and its relevance to the marketplace. It is also the master display on which future trade show stands will be based.

ICI Americas hat dreizehn verschiedene Niederlassungen. Zweck der Ausstellung war es auch, jede mit einem eigenen Display auszustatten und somit alle zu verbinden. Die Displays wurden ergänzt durch eine speziell in Auftrag gegebene Multimedia-Installation, einschließlich eines Films über den von ICI gesponserten Rennwagen. Das komplette Ensemble bietet einen Überblick über die Aktivitäten der Firma und ihrer Bedeutung am Markt. Gleichzeitig dient es als Modell, auf dem zukünftige Messestände basieren werden.

Applying a diagonal grid to the rectangular exhibit space creates visual interest and linking contrasts between different sectors of the whole.

Ein diagonales Raster im rechteckigen Ausstellungsraum schafft eine interessante Ansicht und verbindet Kontraste zwischen den verschiedenen Bereichen.

Year	**1999**
Location	**Germany**
Launch promotion tour	**Contradiction for Men**
Exhibitor	**Calvin Klein Cosmetics, Wiesbaden**
Concept	**meiré und meiré, Frechen-Königsdorf: Mike Meiré, Dirk Meuleneers**
Video	**Calvin Klein**
Realisation	**Eventsure, Cologne**
Size	**Truck 35 m²**
Photos	**Uwe Spoering, Cologne**

Transport

Bridging the Atlantic

Atlantik-Brücke

Imagination for Ford USA

Imagination für Ford USA

The bridge both as a metaphor and a means of communication, transport and connection is well established. But to use the metaphor well requires fluency and grace. The London-based design group have created numerous stand designs for Ford of Europe over recent years, and were invited by Ford USA to create their stand for the Detroit Autoshow in 1999, the most prestigious event in the US motoring fair calendar. The requirement was to present all six Ford brands on a shared site: Ford itself, Mercury, Lincoln, Masda, Jaguar and Aston Martin.

Die Brücke als Symbol und Zeichen der Kommunikation, des Transports und der Verbindung ist allseits bekannt. Um dieses Symbol aber treffend einzusetzen, bedarf es Geschick und Anmut. Die in London niedergelassene Design Gruppe Imagination hatte in den vergangenen Jahren bereits mehrere Stände für Ford Europa entworfen und wurde von der Muttergesellschaft Ford USA eingeladen, deren Stand für die Detroit Motorshow 1999 zu entwerfen – eines der Top-Ereignisse im Messekalender der USA. Vorgabe war, die sechs wichtigsten Marken – Ford selbst, Mercury, Lincoln, Mazda, Jaguar und Aston Martin – auf einer gemeinsamen Fläche zu präsentieren.

The identity of each primary brand area was ensured through an exclusive range of colours, materials and graphic vocabularies.

Die Identität jedes Marken-Bereiches wurde durch entsprechend unterschiedliche Farben, Materialien und Typografie gewährleistet.

Each brand targets a different market, but all are part of the Ford offer: individuality had to become part of the whole. The solution adopted by Imagination was to give each brand an individual space, under a linking bridge. Each area has a co-ordinating colour and detailing that blends into the whole. And the bridge is more than a simple link: it provides a pathway, past a series of concept cars, to the presentation area where new models are unveiled. It is this use of the metaphor that lifts the stand into a special class. The experience of the stand, in other words, is of both diversity and unity, showing the work of Ford as both created and creative.

This richness of inspiration allows the stand, while meeting the main task of presenting the current range, to introduce wider contexts: about Ford's place in the motor industry, about the company commitment to wider issues, especially regarding pollution and safety. The elegance of the overall presentation of the stand allows these matters to be introduced without forcing them.

While the details of graphics, colour co-ordination and lighting throughout the stand are at a level rarely seen in American exhibits, it is not these factors alone that create the special quality of the stand. It is its integrity and integration, the resolution of a complex brief into a coherent whole.

Jede Marke hat eine andere Zielgruppe, dennoch sind sie alle Teil des Ford Angebots: Individualität muß ein Teil des Ganzen werden. Der Lösungsansatz von Imagination bestand darin, jeder Marke eine eigene Fläche unter der Brücke zu geben, welche ihrerseits über dem Stand zur Präsentationsfläche führte. Jede Marke besitzt ihre persönliche Material- und Grafikpalette, die sie mit keiner der anderen Marken teilt: Jaguar zum Beispiel ist Holz, Leder und Chrom zugeordnet. Dadurch wird die Brücke mehr als nur ein Verbindungsglied: Sie ist der Pfad, der, vorbei an Konzeptwagen zur Präsentationsfläche führt, wo die neuen Modelle enthüllt werden. Mit anderen Worten: anhand der Brücke kann der Stand das Erleben von Unterschied und Einheitlichkeit vermitteln, können die Ford-Produkte sowohl im fertigen als auch im Entwicklungsstadium gezeigt werden.

Neben der Präsentation der aktuellen Produktpalette werden auch weiterreichende Kontexte vorgestellt: Die Position von Ford in der Motorindustrie, das Engagement des Unternehmens hinsichtlich Themen wie Umweltverschmutzung und Sicherheit. Die Eleganz der gesamten Präsentation erlaubt es, diese Punkte unaufdringlich einzubinden.

Obwohl Grafik, Farbkoordination und Beleuchtung schon auf einem hohen Niveau sind, gibt es noch andere Merkmale, welche die Qualität des Stands hervorheben: Integrität und Integration, die Abwicklung eines komplexen Auftrags zu einem zusammenhängenden Ganzen.

The design uses the bridge
(above) as a visual link and
a pathway to the projection
area (following page). The
bridge is built to motorway
engineering specifications:
similar attention to detail
goes into individual displays
(right).

Der Entwurf nutzt die
Brücke (oben) als visuelles
Verbindungsstück und als
einen Übergang zum Pro-
jektionsbereich (nächste
Seite). Die Brücke wurde
unter autobahntechnischen
Bedingungen gebaut; mit
ähnlicher Genauigkeit werden die Details der einzelnen Auslagen dargestellt
(rechts).

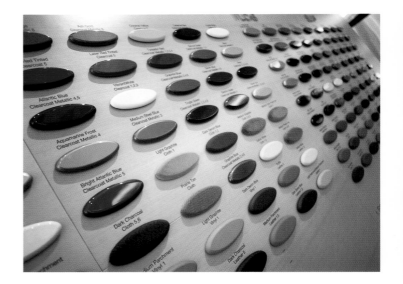

Year	**1999/2000**
Location	**Detroit**
Trade Fair	**Detroit Motor Show**
Exhibitor	**Ford Motor Company**
Concept	**Imagination Ltd.**
Design team	**Adrian Caddy, Douglas Broadley, Francis Court, Raymond Yip, Jason Claisse**
Lighting	**Mike Sobotniki (Imagination)**
Realisation	**Exhibitworks**
Size	**7,750 m²**
Photos	**Imagination Ltd.**

Class of its Own

Eine Klasse für sich

Kauffmann Theilig & Partner
for Mercedes-Benz

Kauffmann Theilig & Partner
für Mercedes-Benz

Motor fairs are special events, attracting enormous public and press attention (proof, if such were needed, of the modern love affair with the motor car.) The launch of a new luxury model is therefore doubly special, and needs the right setting. When Mercedes-Benz (now part of the newly-named and newly-formed DaimlerChrysler group) were looking to launch the new S-Class saloon, they selected the 1998 Paris Motor Show as the venue, and architects Kauffmann Theilig & Partner together with the communication agency Atelier Markgraph as their designers.

The designers realised that a static presentation alone would not convey all the necessary elements, and so planned a dual-purpose stand. The same area, dominated by a curling red wooden waveform, would be both showroom and theatre.

Automobilmessen sind etwas Besonderes. Sie ziehen die Aufmerksamkeit von Bevölkerung und Presse auf sich – ein Beweis, für unsere moderne Liebesbeziehung zum Automobil. Die Enthüllung eines neuen Luxusmodells ist deshalb doppelt so spannend und verlangt nach dem passenden Umfeld. Als Daimler-Benz (heute DaimlerChrysler) beschloß, die neue S-Klasse der Marke Mercedes-Benz zu enthüllen, wählte das Unternehmen 1998 den Automobilsalon in Paris als Auftakt und die Architekten Kauffmann Theilig & Partner zusammen mit der Kommunikationsagentur Atelier Markgraph als Designer.

Für die Inszenierung war klar, daß eine statische Präsentation nicht alle notwendigen Aspekte zeigen würde. Sie entschieden sich deshalb für ein Standdesign, welches zwei Kriterien erfüllt: Die Ausstellungsfläche, beherrscht von einer wellenförmigen rötlichen Holzform, soll gleichzeitig als Schaufenster und als Theater dienen.

Not quite machina ex-deus,
but a transformation scene
is the key part of the drama necessary to launch a
new car. The blinds roll
down, the lights go up, the
dance begins...

Eine Verwandlungsszene
ist das Schlüsselelement
für die Einführung des
neuen Modells. Die Fahnen
kommen herunter, die
Lichter gehen an, der Tanz
beginnt...

Regularly during the fair day the lighting levels would change
and a dance show replace the fixed display.

The wave image is central to the whole presentation, as a
visual element that can be seen from a distance, as a
metaphor for the continuous renewal, like a tide, of the per-
formances celebrating the new car, and in its colour an echo
of the red carpet unrolled for special visitors.

The architectural elements of the stand alone make an ex-
tremely powerful and positive declaration about the positioning and importance of the new S-class. The formal vocabulary
used is wholly abstract, yet expresses through light and vol-
ume the concepts behind the car.

Während der Messetage ändern sich Licht und Raum regel-
mäßig und die „feste Ausstellung" der Exponate wird durch
eine künstlerische Tanzeinlage ersetzt.

Die Verwendung der Welle ist ein zentraler Aspekt der
gesamten Präsentation. Sie dient als von weitem sichtbares
Erkennungsmerkmal und als Symbol – ähnlich den Gezeiten –
für die ständige Erneuerung der Festivitäten anläßlich des
neuen Modells. Außerdem erinnert sie in ihrer Farbigkeit an
den „roten Teppich", der für Ehrengäste ausgerollt wird.

Allein die architektonischen Elemente des Stands geben
eine äußerst starke und positive Erklärung zum Auftritt der
neuen S-Klasse. Die verwendete formale Ausdrucksweise ist
zwar total abstrakt, drückt jedoch durch Licht und Raumge-
staltung Ideen aus, die hinter dem neuen Automodell stehen.

La Classe S

Première mondiale

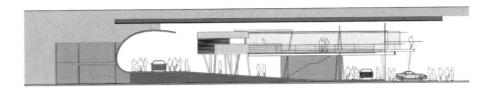

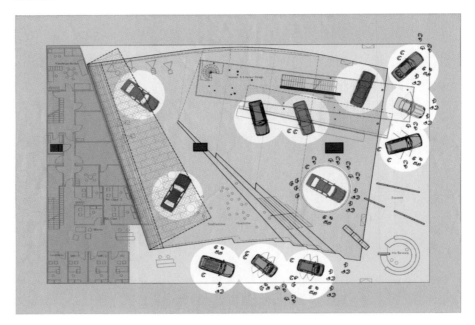

Status exhibition
Section (above),
plan (below)

Zustand Ausstellung
Schnitt (oben);
Grundriß (unten)

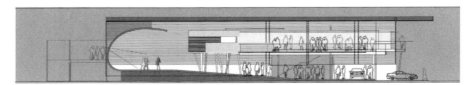

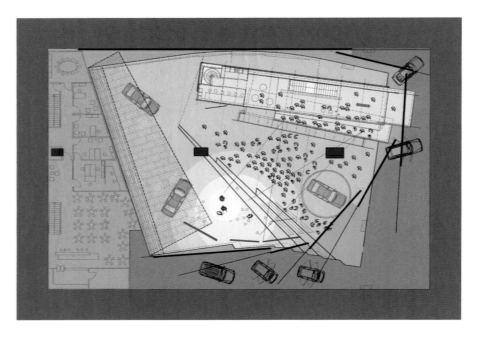

Status show
Section (above),
plan (below)

Zustand Inszenierung
Schnitt (oben);
Grundriß (unten)

Year	**1998**
Location	**Paris**
Trade Fair	**Paris Motor Show**
Exhibitor	**DaimlerChrysler AG, Stuttgart**
Concept	**Atelier Markgraph, Frankfurt;** **Kauffmann Theilig & Partner, Ostfildern**
Architects	**Kauffmann Theilig & Partner** **Freie Architekten BDA: Andreas Theilig, Dieter** **Ben Kauffmann, Rainer Lenz, Manfred Ehrle** **Project Architects: Karen Gerken, Udo Jaschke**
Communication	**Atelier Markgraph, Frankfurt**
Graphics	**Baumann & Baumann, Schwäbisch Gmünd**
Exhibits	**Triad Berlin**
Light Design	**Rolf Derrer: Delux, Zurich**
Realisation	**Ambrosius Messebau, Frankfurt**
Lighting Company	**Sound & Light, Leonberg**
Multi-Media-Performance	**Stephen Galloway - Coreography, Ballett** **Frankfurt - Dance, meso Frankfurt - Sortware,** **Atelier Markgraph - Production**
Size	**1500 m²**
Photos	**Vaclav Reischl, Stuttgart**

Festhalle Festival

Kauffmann Theilig & Partner
for Mercedes-Benz

Kauffmann Theilig & Partner
für Mercedes-Benz

The ideal way to keep the competition away from your stand is to have the hall to yourself. Not that Mercedes-Benz have any need to fear competition, but they regularly take the whole of the Festhalle at the entrance to the Frankfurt show grounds for their stand. For their chosen designers, Kauffmann Theilig & Partner, this creates an architectural opportunity in itself validates the choice of venue. For the 1999 presentation, the exterior windows and skylight dome are blacked out, to create a total environment, which the judges of the iF Exhibition Design Awards dubbed "the Mythos Mercedes" when awarding it Gold.

Die beste Methode Konkurrenz vom eigenen Stand fernzuhalten, ist es, die Halle für sich allein zu haben. Nicht, daß Mercedes-Benz Konkurrenz fürchten müßte, aber in der Regel hat die Marke die gesamte Festhalle am Eingang der Frankfurter Messe für ihren Stand auf der IAA zur Verfügung. Das bedeutet für die beauftragten Architekten Kauffmann Theilig & Partner eine architektonische Herausforderung. Zur Präsentation 1999 wurden die Außenfenster und Oberlichter der Halle komplett abgedunkelt, eine eigene (Licht-) Atmosphäre wurde geschaffen. Überzeugend – urteilten die Jurymitglieder des if exhibition Design Award 1999 und verliehen „dem Mythos Mercedes" einen Gold Award.

The space above the stand
provided the backdrop for
a media landscape of pro-
jected images to reinforce
the central message (right).
The multiple levels allowed
different perspectives on
the stand interior.

Der Raum über dem Stand
bildet die Kulisse für eine
Medien-Landschaft, in der
die projizierten Bilder die
zentrale Botschaft verstär-
ken (rechts). Die vielen
Ebenen lassen verschiedene
Einblicke in das Standesin-
nere zu.

The Festhalle, unlike many halls, has a high ceiling, allowing vertical space to be exploited. Kauffmann Theilig & Partner took full advantage of this, creating together with the communication agencies Triad and Atelier Markgraph a five-storey structure under the dome. From the main entrance foyer an escalator and a stairway, each encased in steel tubes, took visitors to the top floor. From there they would find – like in a museum – their own way through the exhibit, down to the ground floor where every hour a musical and danced performance replaces the turntable display of the latest model. As indoor architecture, the stand is freely-planned, with floors set at angles and recesses, allowing overviews from the higher levels. It is an opportunity for excitement that is exploited to the full.

Kauffmann Theilig & Partner's work for Mercedes-Benz has an assurance and maturity that is, in part, the result of the long collaboration between designer and client. The architects and their communication partners have evolved a wholly visual language for describing the Mercedes-Benz offer, using materials, colour and light to convey product values almost without text. This is architecture and design of a high order.

Im Gegensatz zu den meisten Hallen ist die Festhalle sehr hoch und bietet die Möglichkeit, Raum zu gestalten. Kauffmann Theilig & Partner nutzten diesen Vorteil und schufen zusammen mit den Kommunikationsagenturen Triad und Atelier Markgraph unter der Kuppel eine fünfstöckige Struktur: Vom Haupteingang führen eine Treppe und eine Rolltreppe, in Stahlröhren eingeschlossen, die Besucher nach oben. Von dort finden sie selbst, wie in einem Museum, den Weg durch die Ausstellung nach unten, wo stündlich eine Musik- und Tanzeinlage die Ausstellung der Exponate ablöste. Innenarchitektonisch ist der Stand mit seinen unterschiedlich gewinkelt angelegten Etagen und Nischen freizügig geplant. Er erlaubt Ein- und Überblick aus den oberen Stockwerken. Die erzeugte Raumsituation ist voller Spannung.

Kauffmann Theilig & Partners Arbeiten für Mercedes-Benz sind – teils dank langjähriger Zusammenarbeit zwischen Designer und Kunde – voll Sicherheit und Reife. Die Architekten und ihre Partner aus dem Kommunikationsbereich haben unter Einsatz von Material, Farbe und Licht eine komplett bildhafte Sprache entwickelt, die das Angebot von Mercedes-Benz fast ohne Text beschreiben kann: Design und Architektur höchsten Ranges.

The plan (right) and section
(opposite) show how the
Festhalle offered an opportunity for an extensive and
intricate construction
(above).

Der Grundriß (rechts) und
der Querschnitt (folgende
Seite) zeigen, welche Möglichkeiten sich in der Festhalle für die ausgedehnte
komplizierte Konstruktion
bieten (oben).

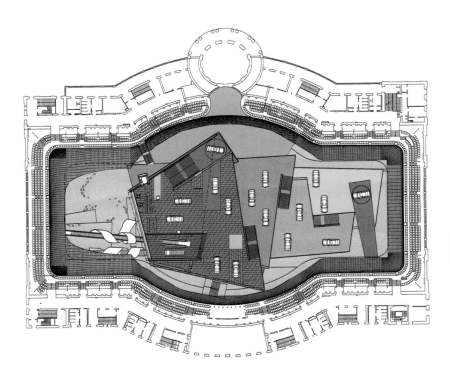

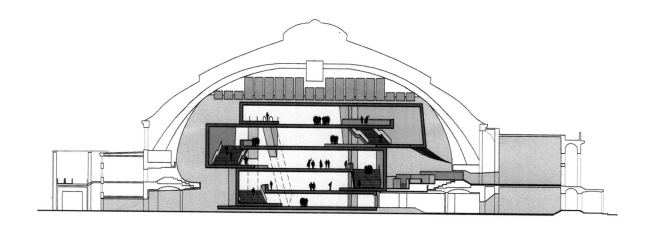

Year	**1999**
Location	**Frankfurt**
Trade Fair	**Frankfurt Motor Show**
Exhibitor	**DaimlerChrysler AG, Stuttgart**
Architects	**Kauffmann Theilig & Partner** **Freie Architekten BDA: Andreas Theilig, Dieter** **Ben Kauffmann, Rainer Lenz, Manfred Ehrle** **Project Architect: Susanne Presser**
Communication concept	**Cooperation Triad, Berlin and** **Atelier Markgraph, Frankfurt**
Graphics, Exhibits	**Cooperation Design³ and spek design,** **Stuttgart**
Lighting	**Delux, Zurich**
Load-bearing construction	**Pfefferkorn & Partner, Stuttgart**
Realisation	**Ambrosius Messebau, Frankfurt**
Lighting Company	**Sound & Light, Leonberg** **Showtec, Köln**
Media	**Mediascreen, Berlin; TV system Electronic,** **Neuffen; XXL Vision, Höchstenbach**
Audio	**Neumann & Müller, Köngen**
Size	**11,500 m²**
Photos	**Roland Halbe, Stuttgart**

Linking the Loop

Verbindungs-Loop

Ingenhoven Overdiek and
Partner for Audi

Ingenhoven Overdiek und
Partner für Audi

The serious purpose (and serious investment) involved in German motor trade fairs is underlined by the fact that the architects Ingenhoven Overdiek & Partner won the commission to design the new Audi stand through an invitational competition. They call the principal element in their design the Loop: it is a freeform curving structure that undulates around the stand.

At first sight this is an odd metaphor for the high-performance, high-technology image of Audi cars, with their specialist applications of four-wheel drive and principle of "vorsprung durch technik." But look more closely at the design of Audi cars themselves, such as the TT Coupé that won a Gold D&AD prize in 1999, and it is in the detail and finish of the curves that its quality is found.

Welche Bedeutung und Investitionsabsichten hinter deutschen Automobilmessen stehen, wird dadurch deutlich, daß die Architekten Ingenhoven Overdiek und Partner nach der Teilnahme an einem Wettbewerb den Auftrag für den Entwurf des neuen Audi Stands auf der IAA 1999 erhielten. Sie nennen das Hauptelement in ihrem Entwurf „Loop": eine kurvige, sich um den Stand schlängelnde Freiform.

Im ersten Moment scheint dies ein seltsames Symbol für das hochtechnisch und hochleistungs-orientierte Image der Marke Audi, ihrer speziellen Anwendung des Vierradantriebs und ihrem Motto „Vorsprung durch Technik". Bei näherem Hinsehen findet man diese Qualität jedoch in den Details und der Formverarbeitung des Audi-Designs wieder, zum Beispiel am TT Coupé, das 1999 mit Gold beim D&AD-Preis ausgezeichnet wurde.

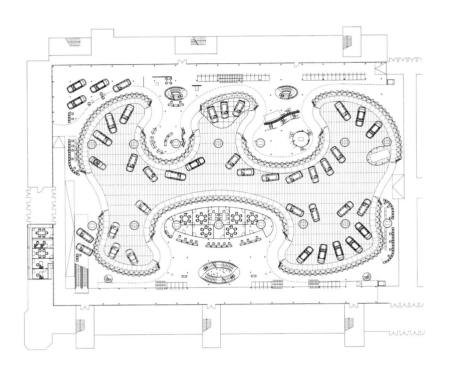

The Loop is such a curve as well, executed in steel, glass and wire rope, and animated by a continually changing light-show that bathes the models on display in different colours. The slightly sloping floor also marks it out as a special space.

The Loop manages both to create individual areas for specific groups of products, while also allowing sufficient overview, through the triangular glass panels of the walls, for the visitor to follow his or her own path. The construction details are elegant, as befits a stand for Audi, and the plan breaks the rectolinearity of traditional fair stand design, as well as encapsulating the underlying design values of the products it presents. Proof that a straight line is not always the right path between two points.

Auch der Loop ist so eine Form, ausgeführt in Stahl, Glas und Drahtseilen, belebt durch eine ständig wechselnde Licht-show, die die Exponate in verschiedenfarbiges Licht tauchen. Zusätzlich betont der leicht angerundete Boden das Besondere dieser Fläche.

Während der Loop individuelle Nischen für die jeweiligen Produktgruppen schafft, können die Besucher, dank ausreichendem Überblick durch die dreieckigen Glasscheiben, ihren eigenen Weg finden. Die Einzelheiten der Konstruktion passen zum Stil von Audi: elegant. Der Grundriß bricht mit dem rechtwinklingen traditionellen Standdesign und reflektiert die grundlegenden Designwerte des präsentierten Produkts. Ein Beweis dafür, daß die gerade Linie nicht immer die beste Verbindung zwischen zwei Punkten ist.

Graphic details show the
consistency of the design
approach: the triangular
glass sections are the basic
building block of the Loop.

Graphische Details zeigen
die Stetigkeit des Designs:
die dreieckigen Glasscheiben dienen als Grundauf-
bauelement für den „Loop".

Year	**1999**
Location	**Frankfurt**
Trade Fair	**Frankfurt Motor Show**
Exhibitor	**Audi AG International Trade Fair, Ingolstadt**
Architect	**Ingenhoven Overdiek and Partner, Düsseldorf**
Communication	**KMS-Team, Munich**
Load-bearing construction	**Werner Sobek Ingenieure, Stuttgart**
Lighting	**Werning Tropp and Partner, Feldafing; Four to one GmbH, Cologne**
Multi-media team	**MediaLab, Munich: Patrick Zenker**
Film, Music	**Velvet, Munich**
Realisation	**Ambrosius Messebau, Frankfurt**
Size	**1st floor 4,880 m² 2nd floor 1,533 m²**
Photos	**H. G. Esch, Cologne**

2,5 I-V6 TDI

Das Audi Highlight auf der IAA

Leistung: 132 kW (180 PS)
Drehmoment: 370 Nm
4-Ventil Technik
Turbolader mit variabler Turbinengeometrie
Radialkolben-Verteilereinspritzpumpe VP 44-S3
Abgasnorm: EU III

Rolling forces
Rollende Kraft

bürlingschindler for
Mercedes-Benz

bürlingschindler für
Mercedes-Benz

The science of forces today is often about analysing the invisible, creating visible but accurate metaphors of invisible events. The stand designer is challenged in the same way to create a three-dimensional enactment of the verbally-expressed positioning and values of a company. Often for these forms to have enough resonance to be widely understood, across countries and cultures, they need to be abstract.

The curving forms of Eckhard Bürling's and Uwe Schindler's stand for Mercedes-Benz at Tokyo have such abstract depth. Do they represent enclosure, projection, movement in space? Are the floating elements roofs, wings or the pathways of energy? The answer, as so often, arises from the whole not the parts.

Wenn heute über Kräfte geforscht wird, geht es oft um die Analyse des Unsichtbaren, um die Erschaffung sichtbarer Metaphern für unsichtbare Ereignisse. Die Herausforderung an den Standarchitekten ist dem vergleichbar: in Worten ausgedrückte Positionen und Werte einer Firma müssen in ein dreidimensionales Format übersetzt werden. Dieses Format muß oft abstrakt angelegt werden, um länder- und kulturübergreifend verständlich und erfolgreich zu sein.

Die kurvigen Formen von Eckhard Bürlings und Uwe Schindlers Stand für Mercedes-Benz in Tokio haben diese abstrakte Tiefe. Repräsentieren sie Eingrenzung, Vorsprung und Bewegung im Raum? Sind die schwebenden Elemente Dächer, Flügel oder Energieströme? Die Antwort ergibt sich, wie so oft, aus dem Ganzen, nicht aus den Einzelteilen.

The dynamic layering of
the upper elements is clear
from the CAD perspective
(right), while the lighting
effects emphasise the horizontality of the finished
stand (above).

Die CAD-Ansicht (rechts)
macht die Dynamik über-
einanderliegender Elemente
deutlich; dagegen betonen
die Lichteffekte die Hori-
zontalen des Standes
(oben).

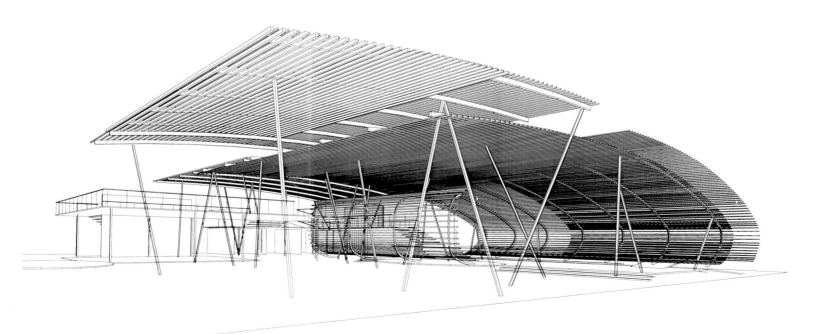

The whole stand has a sense of sleek horizontality and motion in contrast to the static totems of conventional designs.

The lighting effects mark out these dynamic, sculptural elements with clarity (the lighting on the cars themselves is somewhat softer.)

The use of aluminium for the stand design creates a sense of authority and power and echoes the curving lines of the cars themselves, many of which were in a silver finish. Red timber walkways and floor areas, and black carpets, provide a sombre note of contrast. But the handling of design detail lifts the mood, away from heavy engineering towards energetic economy and spatial excitement. The sweep of the architecture itself conveys the idea of safety, control and speed, key elements for the Mercedes-Benz brand.

Der gesamte Stand vermittelt ein Gefühl geschmeidiger Horizontalität und Bewegung, im Gegensatz zu den statischen Totempfählen konventionellen Designs. Klar markieren die Lichteffekte diese dynamischen Skulpturelemente. (Die Beleuchtung der Autos ist etwas weicher.)

Der Einsatz von Aluminium verleiht dem Stand zum einen Autorität und Kraft, zum anderen spiegelt er die kurvigen Formen der meist silbern lackierten Autos wieder. Roter Holzboden und ein schwarzer Teppich geben dem Ganzen eine dunklere Kontrastnote. Diese wird jedoch durch den Umgang mit Designdetails wieder angehoben, weg von der nüchternen Technik hin zu energetischer Wirtschaftlichkeit und räumlicher Spannung. Die schwungvolle Architektur vermittelt die Idee von Sicherheit, Kontrolle und Geschwindigkeit: Schlüsselelemente eines Mercedes-Benz.

Year	**1999**
Location	**Tokyo**
Trade Fair	**33rd Tokyo Motor Show**
Exhibitor	**DaimlerChrysler AG, Stuttgart**
Concept	**bürlingschindler, Stuttgart:** **Gert Schlumberger – Project Architect**
Graphics	**Baumann & Baumann, Schwäbisch Gmünd**
Load-bearing construction	**Ingenieurbüro Dietmar Kirsch, Stuttgart**
Lighting	**Rolf Derrer: Delux, Zurich;** **TLD Lichttechnik GmbH, Wendlingen**
Communication	**ON AIR PRODUCTION, Wiesbaden**
Realisation	**Display International, Würselen**
Size	**approx. 1,600 m²**
Photos	**Andreas Keller, Kirchentellinsfurt**

light
right
Ansorg
Licht in
Stimmung
in the right
light

Licht in
Stimmung
in the right
light
Ansorg
Licht in
Stimmung
in the right
light

Ansorg creates
lighting concepts
for architecture,
retail areas and offices.

n

Licht in
Stimmung
in the right
light
Ansorg
Licht in
Stimmung
in the right
light

Jede neue **Aufgabe** fordert
zu individuellen
Lichtlösungen
heraus.

Ansorg designs
plans and produces
high quality
lighting fixtures.

Lifestyle

Action Stations for Play

Spiel ohne Grenzen

root. for Sony Playstation

root. für Sony Playstation

Computer fair shows are a maelstrom of images: Lara Croft`s improbable bust and Buzz Lightyear's equally pneumatic chin and grin have leapt off the screen to decorate the aisles at every turn. How to make a less superficial statement, especially for the market leader, Sony Playstation? root. design`s brief for ECTS in London in 1998 and 1999 was to reflect game playing as a social experience open to all, and present the values of the brand in an informative and entertaining way.

Computermessen sind ein Strudel von Bildern: Lara Crofts unglaubliche Oberweite und Buzz Lightyears pralles Kinn und Grinsen springen vom Bildschirm und dekorieren die Gänge an jeder Ecke. Wie macht man da eine bedeutungsvolle Aussage, besonders als der Marktführer Sony Playstation? root. designs Aufgabe war es, auf der ECTS in London 1998 und 1999 zu zeigen, daß Computerspiele als soziale Erfahrung offen sind für alle und dadurch den Wert der Marke auf eine informative und unterhaltsame Weise präsentieren.

root. chose two strategies to achieve this. Firstly they commissioned a series of photographs, by Daniel Burn-Forti, of people of all ages playing games on Playstation. These were displayed as halo-illuminated panels around the exhibition area, accompanied by images fom Sony`s current advertising campaigns. This was in addition to a range of monitor`s displaying the new games.

The second strategy was to change the tone. Many game stands (including some earlier Sony stands) favour dark interiors and heavy rock music to emphasise the sense of adventure. root. opted for white walls, soft colours and classical music. (In the 1999 stand this became more formalised again, with an entrance, corridor to the main area of the stand to mark the change of pace. This solution is a statement of social space. It also subtly emphasises that the market leader can choose their own ground, and break general trends with impunity. Less can be more.

root. wählte zwei Wege zur Umsetzung: Zuerst beauftragten sie Daniel Burn-Forti, eine Photoserie zu machen, und zwar von Personen aller Altersgruppen beim Spielen an einer Playstation. Diese Photos wurden auf halogen-beleuchteten Tafeln rund um die Ausstellungsfläche aufgehängt, flankiert von Abbildungen der aktuellen Sony Werbekampagne. Zusätzlich zeigten eine Reihe von Terminals die neuen Spiele.

Als zweites führten sie eine neue „Stimmung" ein. Messestände dieser Art (einschließlich einiger ehemaliger Sony-Stände) sind normalerweise in dunkler Innenausstattung und harter Rockmusik gehalten, um ein Abenteuergefühl zu erzeugen. Dagegen entschied sich root. für weiße Wände, sanfte Farben und klassische Musik. 1999 wurde das durch einen extra Eingangskorridor zur Hauptausstellungsfläche noch mehr betont. Diese Lösung ist eine Aussage zum Raum in unserer Gesellschaft. Gleichzeitig betont sie auf eine subtile Art, daß der Marktführer seinen eigenen Weg gehen und ungestraft aus gängigen Trends ausbrechen kann. Weniger ist manchmal mehr.

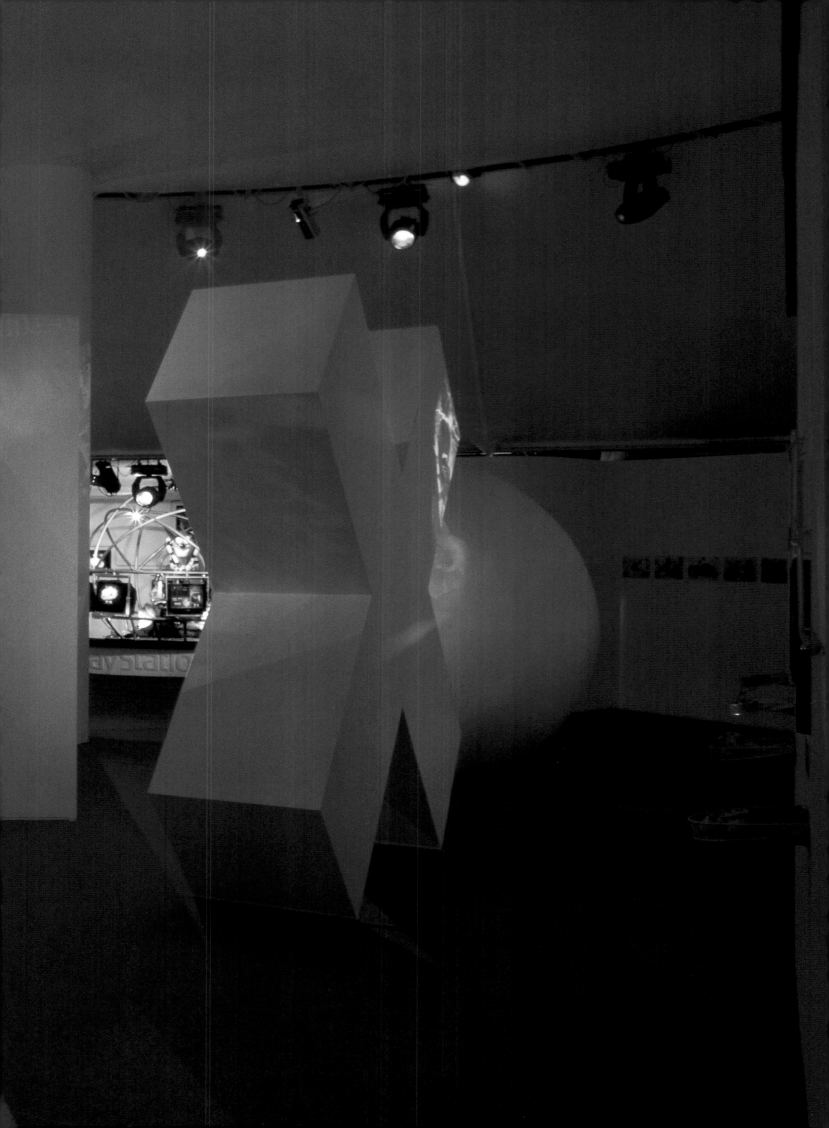

PlayStation®

The formal entrance to the
stand (above) with its cool,
minimal graphics, relaxes
into more fluid forms within (right.)

Der offizielle Eingang zum
Stand (oben) mit seiner
kühlen minimalistischen
Grafik löst sich innen in
fließendere Formen auf
(rechts).

Year	**1998/1999**
Location	**London**
Trade Fair	**ECTS**
Exhibitor	**Sony Playstation Europe**
Concept	**root.**
Realisation	**mice**
Size	**5000 m²**
Photos	**mice**

Let in the Light

Laß das Licht rein

Dieter Thiel
for Ansorg

Dieter Thiel
für Ansorg

The revolution in lighting technology of the last fifteen years has created a bewildering range of choices for the end user. Ansorg have met this by offering a professional design service as well as producing light fittings. At Euroshop 1999 they invited Dieter Thiel to design their stand.

Thiel understood that the best way to understand complexity was through simplicity, and so produced a classic square stand with display areas on the outer edge and meeting rooms flanking the entrance and reception area. The large interior open space allowed a variety of light effects to be demonstrated, while the fittings themselves were shown in the display areas. This balanced the two parts of Ansorg's business, as well as demonstrating the quality of their product, especially the new spotlights and track systems exhibited, and their Power Time control system.

Die seit rund fünfzehn Jahren anhaltende, rasante Entwicklung der Licht-Industrie stellt für den Kunden eine verwirrende Vielfalt dar. Der Leuchtenhersteller Ansorg begegnet dieser Vielfalt – zusätzlich zur Herstellung von Fassungen – mit einem professionellen Designservice. Für die Euroshop 1999 luden sie den Designer Dieter Thiel ein, ihren Stand zu entwerfen.

Thiel war klar, daß der beste Weg, die Komplexität verständlich zu machen, in Schlichtheit bestand. Er kreierte daher einen klassischen, viereckigen Stand mit Schauflächen an der Außenkante und Konferenzräumen rechts und links der Eingangs- und Empfangsfläche. Der große freie Innenraum zeigt eine Vielzahl von Lampen, die Fassungen selbst sind in den Schaukästen ausgestellt. Dadurch werden die beiden Produktbereiche von Ansorg ausbalanciert. Ein besonderes Augenmerk galt den neuen Spotlights und Schienensystemen sowie dem „Power Time controll system".

Ansorg

Licht in
Stimmung
in the right
light

Ansorg

Licht in
Stimmung
in the right
light

Ansorg designs
plans and produces
high quality
lighting fixtures.

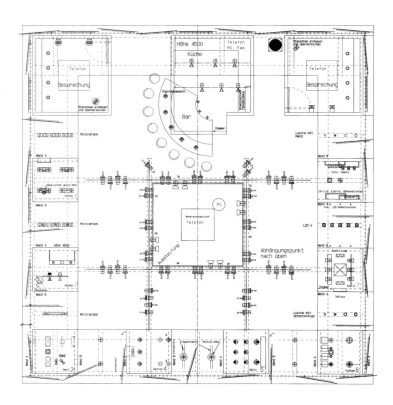

The elegance in Thiel's solution shows through in the minimal number of props he has used: a chair or two by Philippe Starck, a portrait photograph by August Sander. Another subtle touch is the use of frosted glass panels for the outside walls, often set at a couple of degrees to the wall plane, and lit by a battery of downlighter spots.

Die Eleganz von Thiels Lösung zeigt sich in der geringen Anzahl von Extras, die er benötigt: ein oder zwei Stühle von Philippe Starck, ein Portraitphoto von August Sander. Subtil gestaltet sind auch die Außenwände: aus Milchglas, oft ein paar Grad von der Wand abgesetzt, und von Niedervolt-Strahlern beleuchtet.

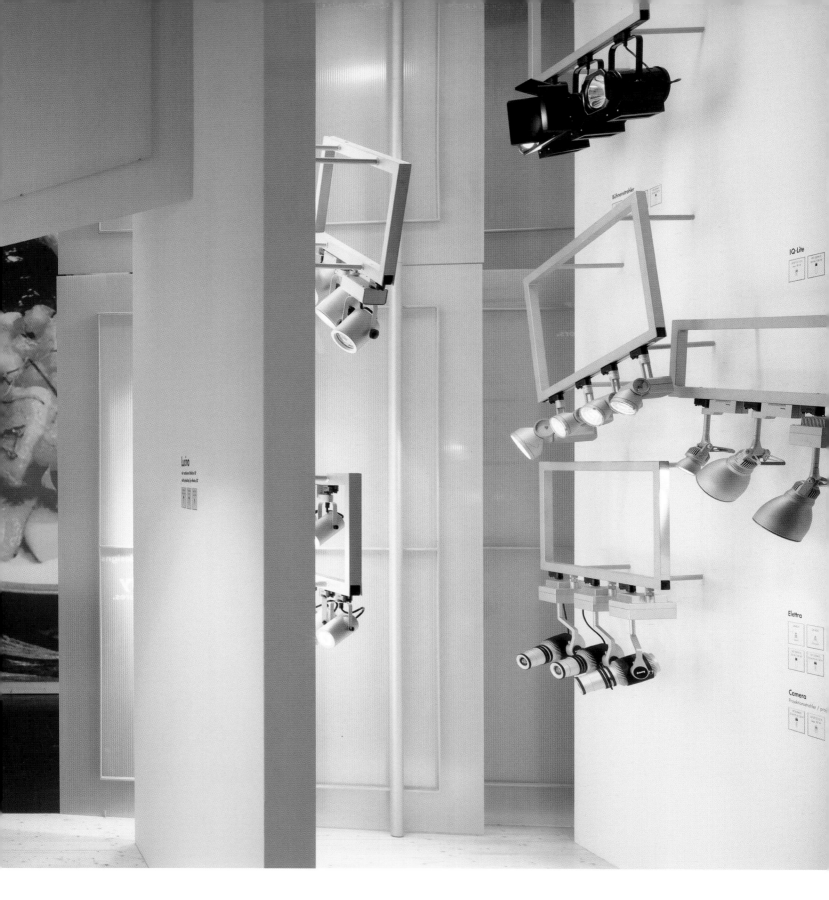

Year	**1999**
Location	**Düsseldorf**
Trade Fair	**EuroShop**
Exhibitor	**Ansorg GmbH, Mülheim**
Architect	**Dieter Thiel, Basle**
Lighting Designer	**Marion Meckel: Ansorg**
Music	**Bohse**
Graphics	**Ansorg; Bangert**
Realisation	**Wolfgang Kunzweiler, Weil am Rhein**
Size	**306 m²**
Photos	**H. G. Esch, Cologne**

Soft Shoe Shuffle

d'art Design Gruppe
for Gabor

d'art Design Gruppe
für Gabor

Archaeologists tell us that even the ancient Romans wore decorated shoes: footwear has been fashion ever since, and still is. Gabor is a family business that sells its ranges of fashion shoes worldwide. They had previously used four individual spaces at the GDS show, but for their fiftieth birthday year in 1999 wanted to bring these into one 1,000 square metre stand, and asked d'art Design to create the stand.

An aisle divided the site into different areas: for product presentation, communication and image. These areas attracted visitors due to changing action within them. The overall aim, in the words of Jürgen Erfling, Head of Advertising, at Gabor, was to "document our leadership in the market and the image value of the product, and to present the innovative approach of the company".

Von Archäologen weiß man, daß selbst die alten Römer dekorierte Schuhe trugen: Seither gibt es die Schuhmode. Gabor ist ein Familienunternehmen, das seine Schuhkollektion weltweit verkauft. Bis 1999 war die Standfläche von Gabor in vier Einzelflächen geteilt. Anläßlich des fünfzigsten Firmenjubiläums sollten diese Flächen auf einem 1000 Quadratmeter großen Stand zusammengeführt werden. Der Designauftrag ging an d'art Design.

Ein Gang teilt die Standfläche in einen Produktpräsentations- und einen Kommunikations- und Imagebereich, der das Publikum durch wechselnde Aktionen anzieht. Jürgen Erfling, Werbeleiter bei Gabor erläutert das Ziel dieses Konzepts: "Unsere Marktführerschaft und den Imagewert der Marke zu dokumentieren und die Innovativität des Unternehmens zu präsentieren."

Zeit Zeichen "50
50 Jahre der Schuh zur Mode   Jahre

Gabor
shoes & fashion

Part of this innovation consists in Gabor offering retailers in Europe "shop and store concepts" for their interiors. This concept had to be integrated, alongside the other trade activities, into the whole stand.

The unity of these elements is achieved through a transparent, minimal case linking the two stand areas, while the supremacy of the product is marked by suspended, sinuously curved sail that extends over the main product presentation area. This area is also at an angle to the aisle, so as to draw the visitor in, while meeting rooms are placed on the outside edges of the stand. The result is a complex whole that unites the different product lines on offer under a common vision of the future of fashion.

Ein Teil dieser Innovation besteht darin, daß Gabor seinen Händlern in Europa ein „shop and store"-Konzept für ihre Innenausstattung anbietet. Dieses Konzept wurde neben anderen Aktivitäten für den Handel in die Standfläche integriert.

Die Verbindung der Standflächen wird durch eine transparente, in der Formensprache reduzierte Hülle aus horizontal verlaufenden Holzstäben erreicht. Die Architektur wird durch ein textiles Band unterstützt, das in einer weich geschwungenen Linie über dem Standbereich abgehängt ist und mittels Bildprojektionen die Markenbotschaft transportiert. Das Ergebnis ist ein komplexes Ganzes, das die verschiedenen Produktlinien unter einer gemeinsamen Vision verbindet.

Year	**1999**
Location	**Düsseldorf**
Trade Fair	**GDS – International Shoe Fair**
Exhibitor	**Gabor Shoes AG**
Concept	**d'art Design Gruppe, Neuss**
Design team	**Jochen Höffler, Guido Mamczur, Conny Cavlek, Klaus Müller, Karin Blanke, Dieter Wolf**
Multi-media team	**d'art Design Gruppe**
Realisation	**ACES, Neuss; CCS, Frankfurt; Zeissig Int. Ausstellungsbau, Springe**
Size	**1,000 m²**
Photos	**H. G. Esch, Cologne**

Lights down low

Ins rechte Licht gerückt

Wolfgang Körber for
Licht Form Funktion (LFF)

Wolfgang Körber für
Licht Form Funktion (LFF)

Bigger does not always mean better. When LFF Leuchten GmbH wanted to show their new co-axial low voltage lighting system at Euroshop 1999 in Dusseldorf, they invited Professor Wolgang Körber to design their whole stand. All thirty-three square metres of it.

LFF stands for Light, Form, Function: the company produces lighting systems using high-end technology (especially in low-voltage modes). The display was to show how different fittings could be fitted to the same low-voltage-lighting-system. Körber's solution was to hang nine CO-AX systems in loops from the top of the stand. This formed a series of arches over a table in the centre of the stand. LFF products were exhibited in display cases all around the stand.

Größer heißt nicht immer besser. Als die Firma LFF Leuchten beschloß, ihr neues coaxiales Niederspannungs-Lichtsystem auf der Euroshop 1999 in Düsseldorf zu zeigen, luden sie Professor Wolfgang Körber ein, den Stand zu entwerfen: 33 Quadratmeter Fläche standen zur Verfügung!

Hinter LFF verbirgt sich „Licht Form Funktion": Die Firma stellt High-Tech-Lichtsysteme her (besonders im Niederspannungsbereich). Die Ausstellung sollte zeigen, wie unterschiedliche Strahlerleuchten an ein Niedervolt-System angeschlossen werden können. In Körbers Umsetzung hängen neun CO-AX-Systeme in Wellenform von der Decke. Dadurch entstehen eine Reihe von Bögen über einem Tisch in der Mitte des Stands. In vitrinenähnlichen Kästen sind rings um den Stand herum Produkte von LFF ausgestellt.

The result is a minimal object of almost excessive elegance: the clear sculptural form echoes the spare design of the CO-AX systems, while the simple colour scheme shows the versatility of the lighting to great advantage. The jury for the iF Awards called the stand "a light object in itself," when giving the design a Gold award.

Das Ergebnis ist ein minimalistisches Objekt von fast übertriebener Eleganz: Die klare, skulpturartige Form der Lichtstruktur gibt das einfache Design des CO-AX-Systems wieder, während das schlichte Leuchtsystem die Vielfältigkeit der Beleuchtung vorteilhaft demonstriert. Die Preisrichter des iF Exhibition Design Award bezeichneten den Stand als „ein Lichtobjekt für sich", als sie ihn mit Gold auszeichneten.

Year	**1999**
Location	**Düsseldorf**
Trade Fair	**EuroShop**
Exhibitor	**Licht Form Funktion Leuchten GmbH, Solingen**
Concept	**Wolfgang Körber**
Graphics	**Wolfgang Körber**
Realisation	**Ueberholz Messebau GmbH, Wuppertal**
Size	**33 m²**
Photos	**Manos Meisen, Düsseldorf**

Neu
Für CDM-TC
Leuchtmittel

Licht **F**orm **F**unktion

Out of Order

Mauk Design for
Levi Strauss & Co.

Mauk Design für
Levi Strauss & Co.

The Magic show in Las Vegas is the main West Coast
menswear fair: Levi Strauss, a brand that originated on the
West Coast used to have a huge booth lost in a back corner.
Many in the business thought the brand, for all its strengths,
had got lost too. For the 1999 show, a new booth and a new
image were needed. Levi Strauss approached Mauk Design
for this.

They proposed what Mitchell Mauk calls "a village." The
meeting rooms and presentation areas are set out on a ran-
dom pattern around a central piazza divided by a sinuous
fretwork wall of wood: "we wanted to avoid the monolithic
straight walls too common at such shows, and above all not
to go for a massive corporate statement." The main use of
the stand was showing clothing in the conference rooms,
while the towers provide a focussed display of clothing,
"making the clothes the heroes."

Die Magic Show in Las Vegas ist die größte Herrenoberbe-
kleidungs-Messe der Westküste: Levi Strauss, eine Marke, die
ursprünglich von der Westküste stammt, hatte jahrelang
einen riesigen Stand, der in einer Ecke verschwand. Viele
Branchenmitglieder waren der Meinung, auch die Marke sei
verschwunden – trotz ihrer Stärke. Für die Messe im Jahr
1999 waren ein neuer Stand und ein neues Image
notwendig. Levi Strauss wandte sich an Mauk Design.

Mitchell Mauk nannte seinen Vorschlag „ein Dorf": Die
Konferenzräume und die Präsentationsfläche sind willkürlich
um eine zentrale Piazza angelegt, welche von einer gewun-
denen, durchlöcherten Holzwand unterteilt wird: „Wir woll-
ten die messeüblichen, monolithisch geraden Wände ver-
meiden und vor allem keine massive Firmenaussage machen."
Hauptsächlich diente der Stand dazu, die Konfektion in den
Konferenzräumen zu zeigen, während die „Türme" eine
gezielte Präsentation des Mottos „Wir machen die Kleider zu
Helden" beinhalten.

The visual complexity of the
stand belies the fact that it
is based on two unit sizes
for the conference and
meeting rooms, so reducing
costs.

Die visuelle Komplexität des
Standes verhüllt die Tat-
sache, daß er zwei Raum-
Einheiten (Konferenz- und
Besprechungs-Räume)
beherbergt. Dadurch werden
die Kosten reduziert.

By breaking the mould in this way, each conference room can be designed to reflect the positioning of the three main ranges of clothing, Vintage, Slates and Dockers, and to create diversity. The press box is a lurid red, the Dockers room a soft grey: another resembles the interior of a cave. Transparent walls, as Mauk says, "turn the business of selling clothes into theatre." Because the buyers can see into the rooms, the layout becomes more accessible, and the excitement builds. The use of continuous design elements (metal framing for the rooms, catwalks and stairs, for example) brings the disparate elements together (as well as keeping costs reasonable), while the graphic support from advertising and commercial imagery reflects the client's positioning.

Though a fifth of the size of the previous stand, the new one was an immediate success (appointment levels were up 50 percent, for example.) The new stand marked a step towards a new approach for the company, both to the fashion world and to its own management: the head of Levi's youth division called the exhibit "the single best implementation of the brand seen to date." As Mitchell Mauk put it "the exhibit went beyond just following fashion to reveling in change."

Durch diese Entwurfsflexibilität kann jeder Konferenzraum so gestaltet werden, daß er die verschiedenen Positionen der drei Hauptkollektionen, „Vintage", „Slates" und „Dockers" widerspiegelt und Abwechslung schafft. Die Pressetribüne ist grell-rot, der Dockers-Raum in sanftem Grau, ein anderer Raum sieht aus wie das Innere einer Höhle. Durchsichtige Wände, sagt Mauk, „verwandeln den Konfektionshandel in ein Theater". Weil der Kunde Einblick in die Räume hat, wird alles leichter zugänglich und die Spannung steigt. Der Einsatz von sich wiederholenden Designelementen (z.B. Metallrahmen für Räume, Laufstege und Treppen) schafft Kontinuität (und hält gleichzeitig die Kosten im Rahmen), während Elemente aus Reklame und Werbespots die Sicht des Kunden auf sich ziehen.

Obwohl er nur noch ein Fünftel so groß ist, wurde der neue Stand sofort ein Erfolg. Die Messetermine steigerten sich um 50%. Es zeichnete sich eine neue Haltung der Firma ab: ein Herantasten an die Modewelt und auch an das eigene Management: Der Chef der Levi's Jugendabteilung nannte die Ausstellung „die bis heute beste Einführung der Marke". Mitchell Mauk stellte fest: „die Ausstellung ging über das reine Mode-Interesse weit hinaus".

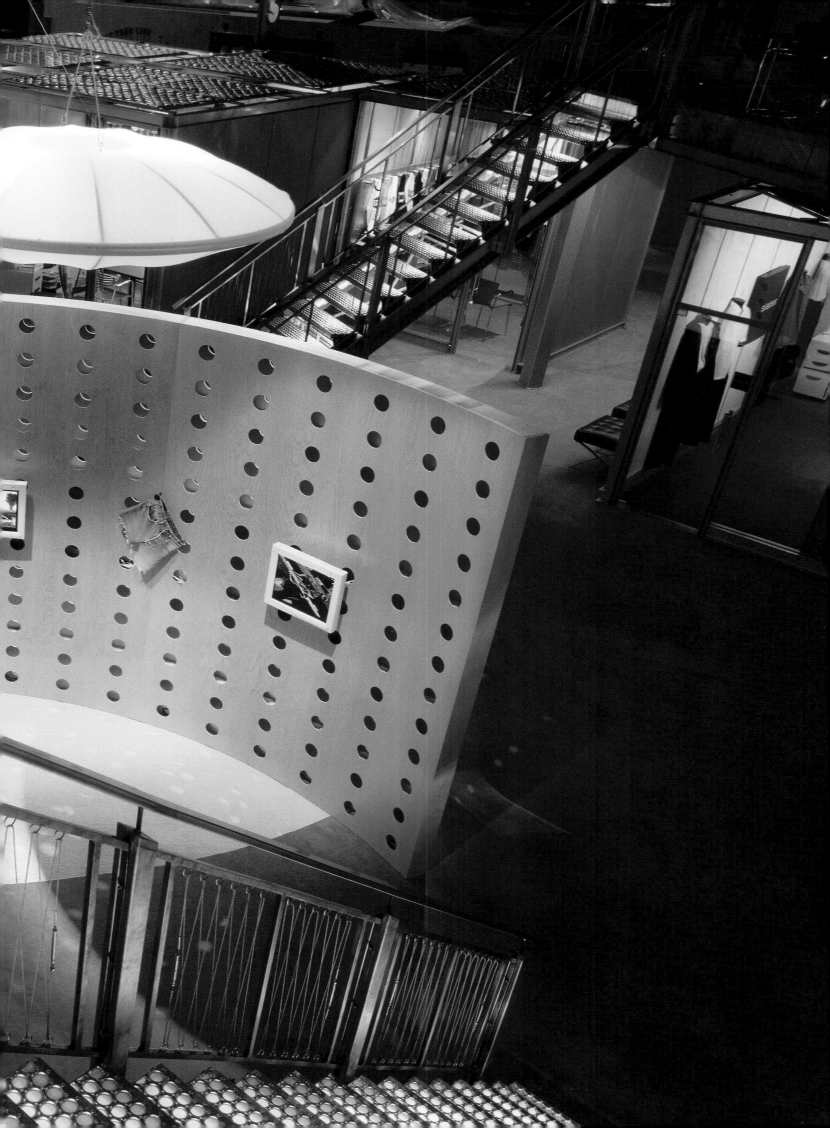

Year	**1999**
Location	**Las Vegas**
Trade Fair	**Magic Show**
Exhibitor	**Levi Strauss & Co.**
Concept	**Mauk Design**
Design team	**Mitchell Mauk, Adam Brodsley, James Pennington-Kent**
Graphics, Communication	**Foote, Cone & Belding**
Realisation	**Pinnacle Exhibits**
Size	**approx. 1,400 m²**
Photos	**Andy Caulfield**

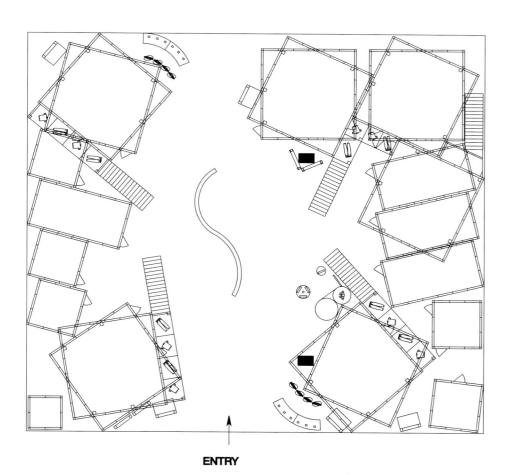

ENTRY

Light on White

Lichtspiele

Arno Design
for Duravit

Arno Design
für Duravit

With designers such as Philippe Starck and Michael Graves working as consultants, Duravit is positioned at the top end of the bathroom equipment market. Their stand at ISH in Frankfurt, 1999, designed by Arno Design, looks in plan very simple: a rectangular stand with a circular conference and meeting area at one end and a grid of wall panels as backdrops for the product range at the other, all finished in white and grey.

A clear and minimal solution, absolutely appropriate for the values of cleanliness and modernity associated with the baths and basins on show, as it seems. But the reality is transformed by the light effects. Gobos pick out brand names and designer's signatures on the outside walls of the conference area, while the whole is washed in a range of changing tones, from blue to red through a range of pinks and purples.

Mit Designern wie Philippe Starck und Michael Graves als Beratern steht Duravit an der Spitze des Markts für Badezimmer-Einrichtungen. Der Grundriß ihres Stands auf der ISH in Frankfurt 1999, entworfen von Arno Design, ist einfach: Ein rechteckiger Stand mit einer kreisförmigen Konferenzfläche an einem, und einem Raster aus Wandtafeln als Hintergrund für die Kollektion am anderen Ende – alles in weiß und grau gehalten.

Eine klare und minimalistische Lösung, absolut passend für die Wertvorstellung von Reinlichkeit und Modernität, die man mit den ausgestellten Wannen und Becken verbindet. Aber diese „reine" Realität wird durch die Lichteffekte verwandelt: Gobos beleuchten Markennamen und Designersignaturen an der Außenwand der Konferenzfläche. Alles wird von einer ständig wechselnden Farbskala überflutet, die von blau bis rot über verschiedene rosa und violett Töne reicht.

The balance of colour is such that the products on display are never completely saturated by the lighting: instead it provides animation and depth to a carefully nuanced showcase for the company's offer.

Die Farbbalance ist so gestaltet, daß die Exponate nie komplett vom Licht durchtränkt sind: Statt dessen gibt das Licht dem sorgfältig differenzierten Schaufenster der Firma Lebendigkeit und Tiefe.

Michael Graves'
dreamscape

DURAV

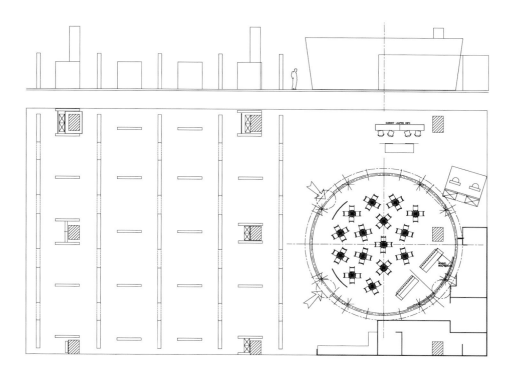

Year	**1999**
Location	**Frankfurt**
Trade Fair	**ISH**
Exhibitor	**Duravit AG**
Concept	**Arno Design, Munich: Peter Haberlander**
Multi-media, Video	**Kaiser & Mohr**
Size	**800 m²**
Photos	**Frank Kotzerke**

Showing a Light

Zeig mir ein Licht

McMillan Group for
Electronic Theatre Controls (ETC)

McMillan Group für
Electronic Theatre Controls (ETC)

Imagine a narrow space of twenty foot by fifty, with a thirty-six foot ceiling. A difficult brief? Not if the client designs lighting systems for the theatrical and architectural markets, as Electronic Theatre Controls do, when they asked the McMillan Group for a modular stand design for the LDI show in Miami.

McMillan used the air space to hang a series of curved white wing shapes over the stand, as surfaces for a projected lightshow. This provided a visual marker for the show, as well as demonstrating in practice the capabilities of the client's lighting and control equipment. Changing coloured patterns and images were projected onto the scrim screens, from eye level up to a height of thirty feet. The control units and lighting systems were connected by a cable raceway.

Man stelle sich einen schmalen Raum von 6 mal 15 Metern mit einer 10 Meter hohen Decke vor. Ein schwieriger Auftrag? Nicht, wenn der Aussteller selbst Lichtsysteme für den Theater- und Architekturmarkt entwirft – so im Fall von Electronic Theatre Controls, der die McMillan Group beauftragte, ein modulares Design für ihren Stand auf der LDI Messe in Miami zu konzipieren.

McMillan nutzte den freien Raum, um eine Reihe von weißen, flügelartigen Formen über dem Stand aufzuhängen, als Leinwand für eine projizierte Lichtshow. Dadurch entstand ein Blickpunkt für die Messe und gleichzeitig eine Projektionsfläche, um die Licht- und Kontrollausstattung des Kunden in der Praxis zu demonstrieren. Wechselnde Farbmuster und Bilder wurden von Augenhöhe bis auf eine Höhe von 9 Metern auf die Baumwoll-Leinwände projiziert. Die Kontrolleinheiten und Lichtsysteme wurden durch eine Kabel-Zuführungsbahn verbunden.

As Charlie McMillan put it "the design challenge was to keep the exhibit open at eye level and create an exhibit overhead that would be a "canvas to paint" with light.

To emphasise the versatility of the client's programmable control equipment, Duane Schuler of the Chicago Lyric Opera was invited to design the lighting scheme at Miami: other well-known theatrical lighting designers will be invited for further trade fairs.

Charlie McMillan meint dazu: „Die Herausforderung bestand darin, die Ausstellung auf Augenhöhe zu halten und darüber noch ein extra Display zu schaffen", eine „Leinwand für Lichtmalerei".

Um die Vielfalt der programmierbaren Kontrollausstattung des Kunden hervorzuheben, wurde Duane Schuler von der Chicago Lyric Opera eingeladen, das Lichtprogramm in Miami zu entwerfen: Andere bekannte Theaterlichtdesigner sollen auf zukünftige Messen eingeladen werden.

Year	**1998**
Location	**Miami**
Trade Fair	**LDI-Lighting Design Show**
Exhibitor	**Electronic Theatre Controls (ETC)**
Concept	**McMillan Group Inc.**
Design team	**Charlie McMillan, Nancy McMillan, John Grasso, Tim Burnham (ETC)**
Lighting	**Duane Schuler, Chicago Lyric Opera**
Realisation	**General Exhibits & Displays**
Size	**92 m²**
Photos	**McMillan Group Inc.**

Teddy Bears' Picnic

Teddybär Picknick

Dietrich Display
for Steiff

Dietrich Display
für Steiff

The market for soft toys has moved out of its traditional domain of products for babies and children into a general gift area. Margarete Steiff GmbH are a long established firm specialising in this field. For their stand at the International Toy Fair 1999 in Nuremberg, they wanted a solution which was to be planned under the economic aspect of reusing the building components. At the same time the stand had to be flexible for the changing range and able to show visitors a new face each year.

Der Markt für Stofftiere hat sich von traditionellen Segmenten wie Baby- und Kinderprodukten gelöst und in Richtung Geschenkartikelmarkt weiter entwickelt. Die Margarete Steiff GmbH ist seit langem in diesem Bereich etabliert. Für ihren Stand auf der Nürnberger Spielwarenmesse 1999 suchten sie nach einem Messeauftritt, welcher unter dem wirtschaftlichen Aspekt des mehrmaligen Einsatzes der Bauteile geplant werden sollte. Gleichzeitig sollte der Stand für das sich verändernde Sortiment flexibel sein und den Besuchern jedes Jahr ein neues Gesicht zeigen.

Changing the display methods for the different groups of objects both provides a link between each category, and also bridges the scale gap between the individual items and the stand as a whole.

Durch verschiedene Displaysysteme entsteht eine zweifache Wirkung: Verbindung zwischen den Produktgruppen und den unterschiedlichen Exponatgrößen.

Dietrich Display chose an arrangement, based on enclosing the stand with suspended fabric walls lit with soft colours and moved animal gobos. Fabric dividers were used in the interior spaces to demarcate products groups. Every product group was allocated a certain fragrance, for example, comforting smells of vanilla and spices aroused childhood memories in visitors in the Classic Department.

A different display systems was also used for each group (open box shelving in white or natural wood, individual black stands, wire suspension constructions and so on.) The same restraint was used in fitting out meeting rooms and the hospitality area, with natural wood chairs and tables that match the plain wooden flooring made of industrial parquet.

 The design solution is both simple to install and highly adaptable. A more decorative approach would have been distracting and inappropriate. The cuddly toys are the main actors of this production. As it is Dietrich's work forms a backdrop for the products that emphasises their quality and market positioning.

Dietrich Display wählte ein Arrangement, das darauf beruhte, den Stand mit hängenden Stoffbahnen einzufassen, die in sanften Farben und mit bewegten Tier-Gobos beleuchtet wurden. Stoff-Trennwände wurden im Innenraum eingesetzt, um die Produktgruppen voneinander abzusetzen. Jeder Produktgruppe wurde ein Duft zugewiesen: z.B. weckten Wohlgerüche nach Vanille und Gewürzen in der Classic-Abteilung Kindheitserinnerungen beim Besucher.

Zusätzlich wurden unterschiedliche Displaysysteme für die einzelnen Produktgruppen verwendet (offene Boxregale in weiß oder Naturholz, individuelle Ständer, hängende Stahlseil-Konstruktionen usw.). Die gleiche Zurückhaltung spürt man in der Einrichtung der Konferenzräume und der Cafeteria: mit Stühlen und abgehängten Lamellen aus Naturholz, passend zum Holzboden aus Industrieparkett.

Die Designlösung ist einfach zu installieren und gleichzeitig leicht anzupassen. Mehr Farbe wäre in diesem Fall unpassend gewesen und hätte abgelenkt. Die Plüschtiere sind die Hauptdarsteller der Inszenierung. Dietrich Design schafft einen Hintergrund für die Produkte, welcher dem hohen Anspruch der Marke gerecht wird.

The design of the hospitality area follows the same reduced and unfussy design vocabulary as the rest of the stand.

Die Gestaltung des Gäste-bereiches zeigt die gleiche reduzierte Designsprache wie der gesamte Stand.

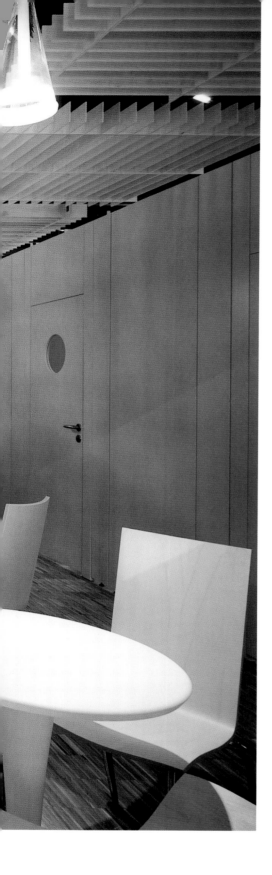

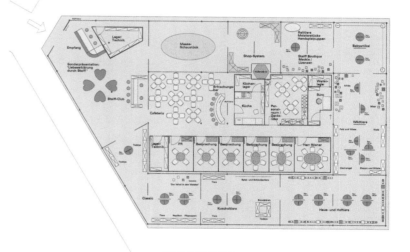

Year	**1999**
Location	**Nuremberg**
Trade Fair	**International Toy Fair**
Exhibitor	**Margarete Steiff GmbH, Giengen**
Concept	**Dietrich Display, Friolzheim: Albrecht Willer – Architect**
Realisation	**Dietrich Display, Friolzheim**
Size	**550 m²**
Photos	**Frank Kleinbach**

Once in a Lifetime

Einmal im Leben

Lorenc + Yoo Design for
Lifetime Movie Network

Lorenc + Yoo Design für
Lifetime Movie Network

The Lifetime Movie Network was launched at the Western Cable Show in Anaheim, California, in 1998. LMN is a new feature film channel intended mainly for a woman's audience. But Lifetime Television, creators of LMN, do not only distribute films, they also make them. The stand design was intended to position the new channel as delivering quality entertainment and information.

To combine the movie making and home viewing aspects. Lorenc+ Yoo Design created two main areas on the stand, a studio space, complete with Panavision camera on a crane, and a "living room" studio set with comfortable armchairs and sofas and a video wall. The crane can rise fourteen feet into the air, so giving a visual cue to the stand at a distance.

Das Lifetime Movie Network wurde auf der Western Cable Show in Anaheim, Kalifornien, 1998 vom Stapel gelassen. LMN ist ein neuer Spielfilmkanal, der sich hauptsächlich an ein weibliches Publikum richtet. Aber Lifetime Television, die Väter von LMN vertreiben nicht nur Filme, sie produzieren sie auch. Das Standdesign sollte den neuen Kanal als Lieferanten von qualitätvoller Unterhaltung und Information etablieren.

Um den Aspekt Filmproduktion mit dem des Heimkinos zu verknüpfen, schuf Lorenc + Yoo Design auf dem Stand zwei Hauptbereiche: einen Studiobereich, komplett mit Panavision Kamera auf einem Kran, und ein „Wohnzimmer"-Filmset mit gemütlichen Sesseln, Sofas und einer Videoleinwand. Der Kran kann bis auf über vier Meter Höhe verlängert werden und gibt so ein weithin sichtbares Wahrzeichen für den Stand ab.

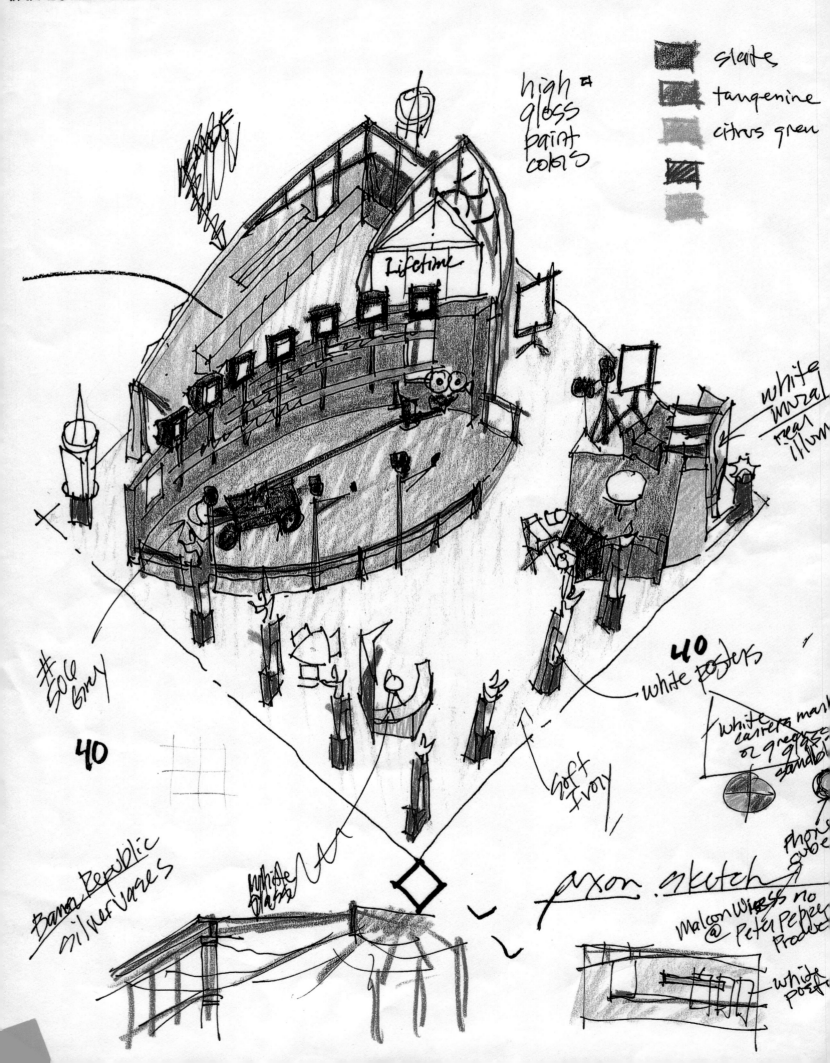

JAN LORENC DESIGN INC. *Lifetime*

high gloss paint colors

slate
tangerine
citrus green

Lifetime

white mural real illum

#506 grey
40

40 white posters

Banana Republic silver vases

soft Ivory

white letters marker or glass standoff

white glass

axon sketch

phone cube

Malcom Wiley no @ Peter Pepper Products

white post

The other main visual feature is the wall backing the studio set, a curving line of rising cherrywood panels with grey text elements and monitors. The same finish is given to the pylons on the outer edge of the stand.

It is this consistency of detail and investment in materials that gives the stand its quality. (The reception desk at the top corner, for example, has a curved glass top that echoes the form of the main wall, and the meeting area behind the studio set also has curved walls.) All the furniture for the stand was designed by Lorenc + Yoo Design. The decision to use curved forms and strong but sophisticated colours marked the stand out as different, and its values matched the product offer of the new network.

Ebenso wichtig ist die Rückwand des Studiobereichs: eine kurvige Linie sich erhebender Kirschbaumholzplatten mit grauen Textelementen und Bildschirmen. Die Masten am Rand des Stands haben dieselbe Oberfläche.

Die Durchgängigkeit bei den Details und dem hochwertigen Material verleiht dem Stand seine Qualität. Die Empfangstheke in der oberen Ecke hat zum Beispiel eine kurvige Glasplatte, welche die Form der Hauptwand aufnimmt. Der Konferenzbereich hinter dem Studio hat kurvige Wände. Alle Möbelstücke für den Stand wurden von Lorenc + Yoo Design entworfen. Was den Stand von anderen abhebt, war die Entscheidung, kurvige Formen und elegante Farben zu verwenden. So gleicht er in der Anmutung dem Produktangebot des neuen Networks.

Lifetime

VISIONARY
Elevating

COMPELLING
Uplifting

INFORMATIVE
aring

HY

NETWORK

3A *Women represent 52% of the world's population. Lifetime Television is cable's most successful female-oriented network. The reason for Lifetime Movie Network is simple: women told us they wanted it.*

LIFETIME MOVIE NETWORK

Lifetime SPORTS
SPORTS

ORK

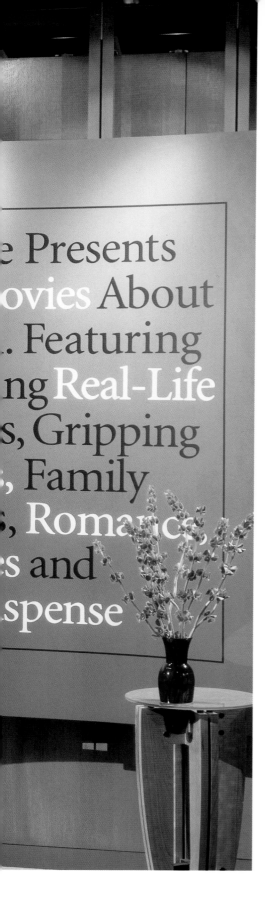

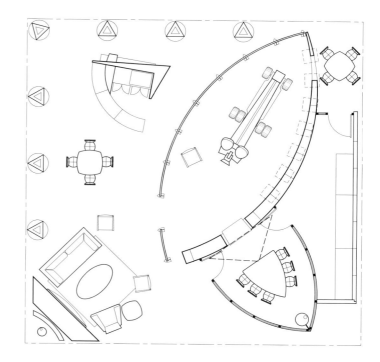

Year	**1998, 1999, 2000**
Locations	**Los Angeles (Anaheim), Atlanta, Dallas**
Trade Fair	**Western Cable Show**
Exhibitor	**Lifetime Television, Lifetime Movie Network launch**
Concept	**Lorenc + Yoo Design**
Design team	**Jan Lorenc – Design Director/ Project Manager, Chung Youl Yoo – Designer, David Park – Designer, Steve McCall – Designer, Janice McCall – Interior Designer, Gary Flesher – Architect**
Lighting	**Ramon Luminence Design: Ramon Noya**
Multi-media team	**Lifetime Television, New York**
Graphic Panels	**Designers Workshop, Chamblee: Lean Seal**
Graphics, Communication	**Factor, Atlanta: Rory Myers**
Realisation	**MDM Scenery Works, Atlanta: Ken McGraw**
Size	**1,600 m²**
Photos	**Rion Rizzo: Creative Sources Photography**

Views in Colour

Farbige Aussichten

Zumtobel Staff
own stand

Zumtobel Staff
Eigenstand

Goethe and Newton agreed on one thing: that without colour light is not worth much. Zumtobel Staff for their stand at Euroshop 1999 set out to agree as well. With dynamic lighting staged by electric light technology and professional lighting systems, worlds of experience were created for the areas of sales and presentation. Dynamic light, colour and changing architecture could all be experienced.

This may seem unsubtle, but it has two major virtues. Firstly it shows how the fittings can create light with the proper colour balance - a key questions in retailing for example. Secondly it portrays Zumtobel Staff as a vibrant and dynamic enterprise.

Goethe und Newton waren sich in einem Punkt einig: Ohne Farbe ist Licht nicht viel wert. Der Zumtobel Staff Eigenstand demonstrierte dieses Plädoyer auf der Euroshop 1999. Dieser Stand war eine Schatzkiste voller Licht und Farbe. Mit dynamischem Licht, elektronischer Lichttechnologie und professionellen Lichtsystemen inszeniert, wurden Erlebniswelten für Verkauf und Präsentationen geschaffen. Licht, Farbe und sich verändernde Architektur waren erlebbar.

Das mag im ersten Moment plump klingen, hat aber zwei große Vorteile. Erstens sieht man, wie die Leuchten Licht mit der richtigen Farbbalance erschaffen – ein wichtiger Verkaufspunkt. Zweitens wird Zumtobel Staff als ein lebendiges und dynamisches Unternehmen dargestellt.

Formal games with shapes
and light are relieved by
the introduction of natural
and curved forms within
the display cases.

Strenge Spiele mit Licht
und Schatten werden
durch die natürlichen ge-
schwungenen Formen in
den Schaukästen aufge-
lockert.

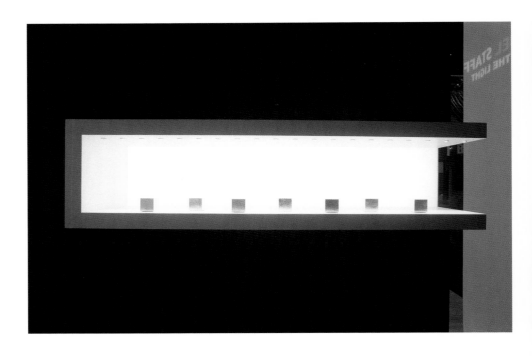

Year	**1999**
Location	**EuroShop**
Trade Fair	**Frankfurt**
Exhibitor	**Zumtobel Staff, Dornbirn**
Concept	**Zumtobel Staff, Dornbirn**
Size	**240 m²**
Photos	**Dirk Sondermann**

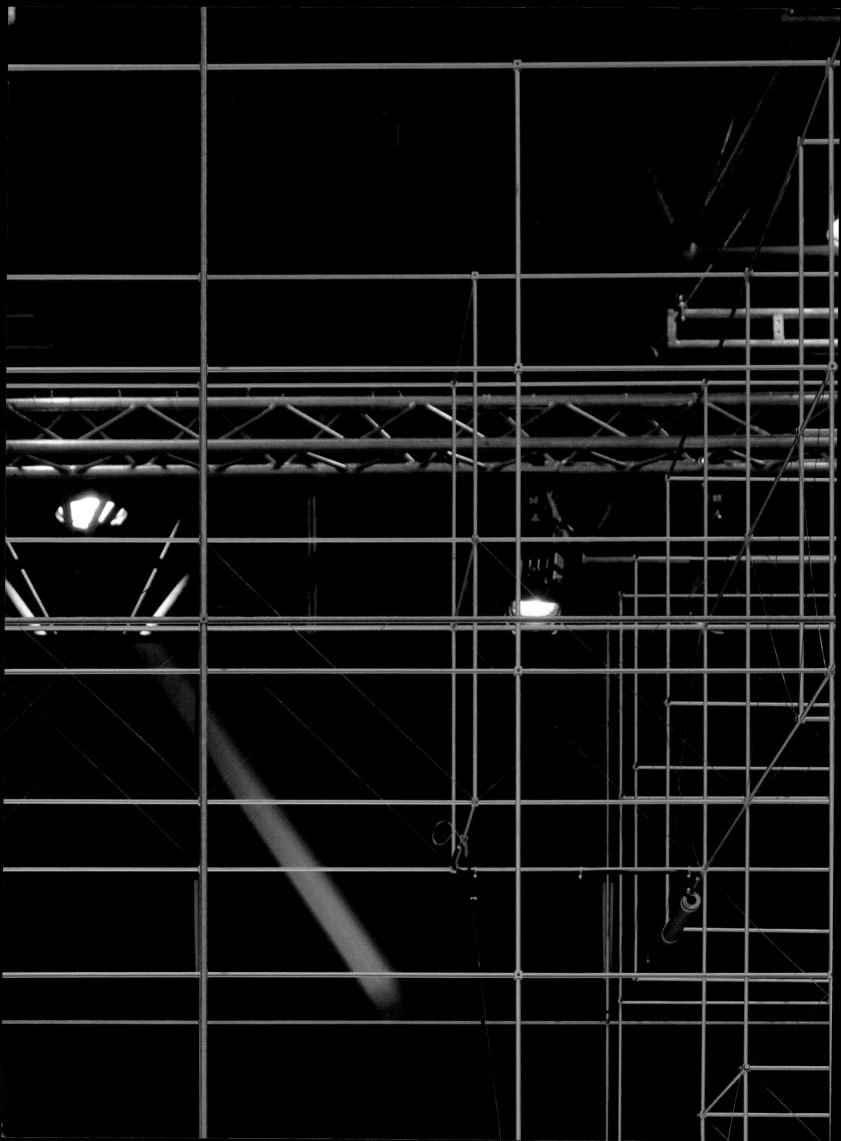

Business to Business

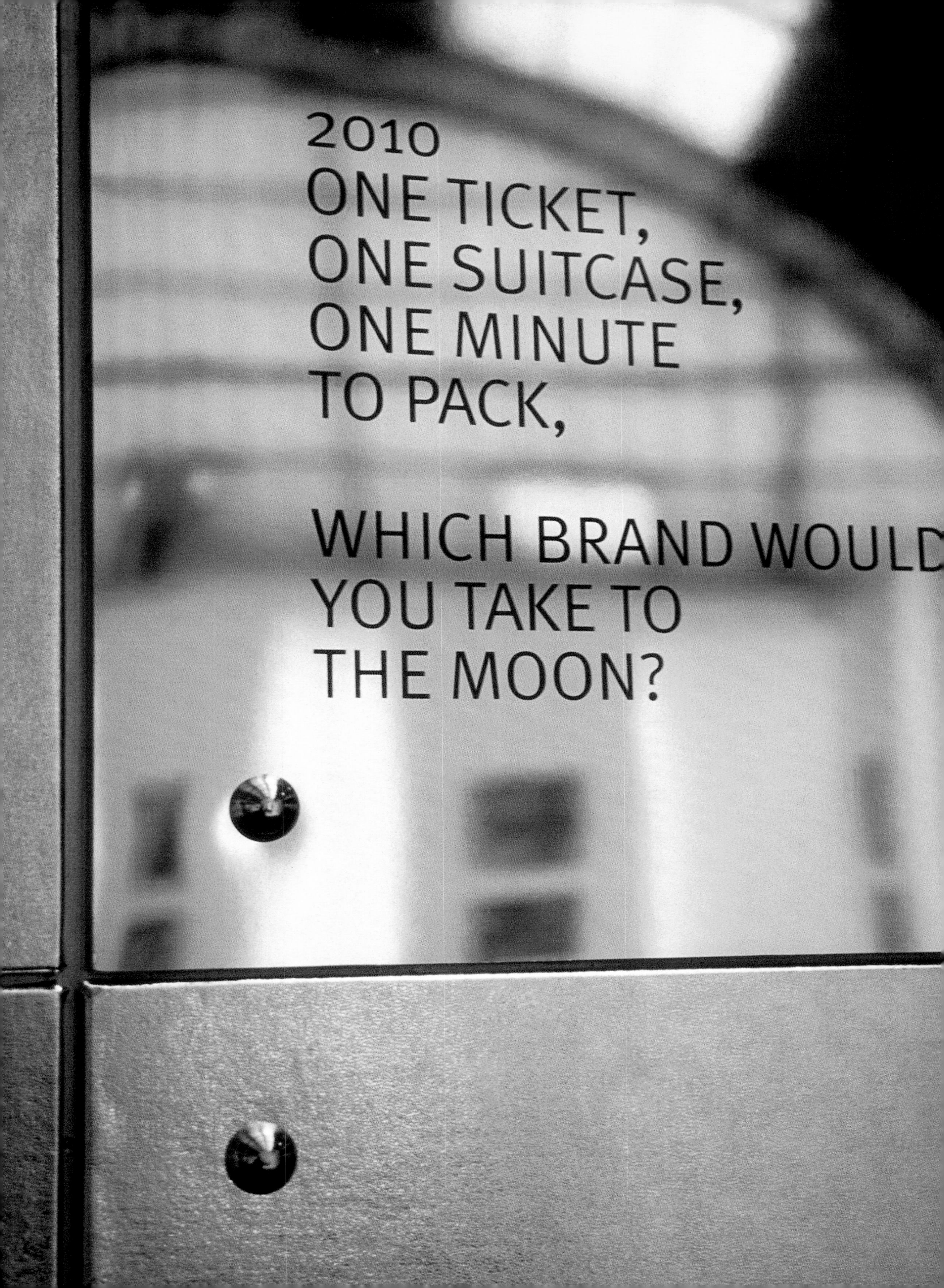

2010
ONE TICKET,
ONE SUITCASE,
ONE MINUTE
TO PACK,

WHICH BRAND WOULD
YOU TAKE TO
THE MOON?

Moon Dreams

Mondträume

Enterprise IG
own stand

Enterprise IG
Eigenstand

How does a design company tell the professional world about itself in a new and original way? Brochures can list clients and awards, CD-ROMS feature exciting visual solutions, press articles showcase particular projects, but how to encapsulate the ethos, attitudes and competence of a design consultancy, within a small stand at a business to business show? This was the challenge for Enterprise IG, the branding consultancy based in London that is part of the international WPP group.

Enterprise IG decided that serious fun was the right approach. Imagine, they suggested, that you have one minute to pack the one suitcase you can take on a trip to the Moon in 2010. Which brands would you take? This was the question they put to everyone in the office, both in design and marketing.

Wie präsentiert sich ein Designstudio auf eine neue und originelle Weise der Fachwelt? In Broschüren kann man Kunden und Auszeichnungen aufführen, CD-ROMs zeigen spannende optische Lösungen, Presseberichte beleuchten spezielle Projekte. Aber wie fängt man Glaubwürdigkeit, Standpunkte und Kompetenz eines Designberatungsbüros ein, um sie auf einem kleinen Messestand Geschäftsleuten zu demonstrieren? Mit dieser Herausforderung sah sich Enterprise IG, das Londoner Beratungsbüro für Markenentwicklung und Mitglied der internationalen WPP Gruppe, konfrontiert.

Enterprise IG war der Meinung, daß seriöse Unterhaltung der richtige Ansatz sei. Man stelle sich zum Beispiel vor, man hat nur eine Minute, um den einzigen Koffer zu packen, den man 2010 auf eine Reise zum Mond mitnehmen darf. Welche Markenartikel soll man einpacken? Diese Frage wurde an jeden Mitarbeiter in Design und Marketing gestellt.

FLIGHTS OF FANCY

The chosen six were exhibited in specially configured aluminium flight cases within the metallic box that was the stand. The selected brands included a Vespa scooter, Evian mineral water, the Royal and Ancient Golf Course at St Andrews in Scotland, Nike shoes, Tupperware containers and a Kodak disposable camera. Each was accompanied by text by the person who had selected it. The whole thing was light-hearted, intended as an entertaining point of focus in a busy show. But it had a serious purpose behind it, to show that the company could react with creativity, wit and personality to any situation. There was a serious challenge in the brief here too, with its suggestion that if we could start again on the Moon, only bringing the best.

The stand succeeded in making a different statement from the more formal proposals offered by other design companies, and was certainly popular with visitors. So popular that after the show ended, someone stole the whole display!

Sechs der Antworten wurden ausgewählt und in speziell angefertigten Aluminiumkoffern in der Metallbox, die als Stand diente, ausgestellt. Die ausgewählten Markenartikel waren z.B.: Ein Vespa Roller, Evian Mineralwasser, der Royal and Ancient Golf Course in St. Andrews in Schottland, Nike Schuhe, Tupperware Dosen und eine Kodak Einwegkamera. Zusätzlich gab es einen Begleittext der Person, die den Artikel ausgewählt hatte. Die Idee war zwanglos, als unterhaltsamer Brennpunkt auf einer geschäftigen Messe gedacht. Aber sie hatte einen ernsten Hintergrund: Sie zeigte, daß die Firma kreativ, witzig und mit Persönlichkeit auf jede Situation reagieren konnte. Gleichzeitig forderte sie auf zu der Überlegung, daß wir, wenn wir auf dem Mond noch mal von vorn anfangen könnten, nur das Beste bringen sollten.

Die Aussage des Stands setzte sich erfolgreich von den förmlicheren Vorschlägen anderer Designfirmen ab. Sie war vor allem bei den Besuchern sehr beliebt. So beliebt, daß jemand, als die Messe vorbei war, alle sechs Ausstellungsstücke gestohlen hat.

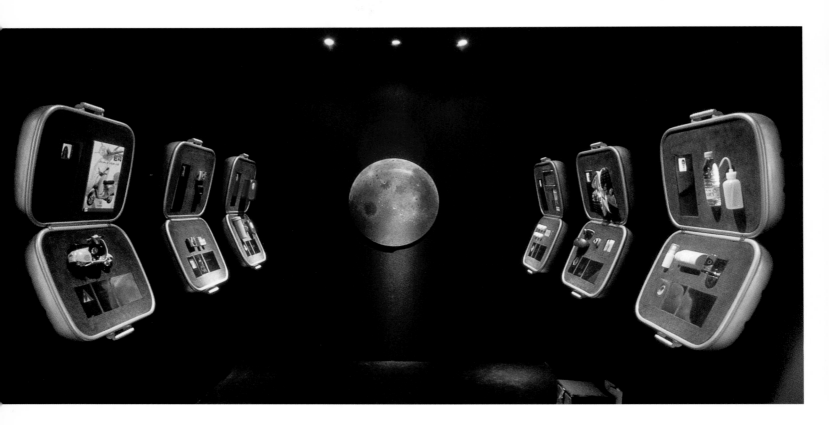

The moon image at the
end of the small stand
(above) is also a window
for those outside to see in.

Durch den Mond am Ende
des Stands läßt sich auch
von außen hereinschauen.

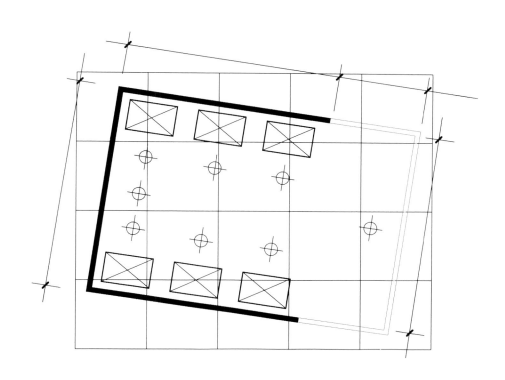

Year	**1999**
Location	**London**
Trade Fair	**The Design Show**
Exhibitor	**Enterprise IG**
Concept	**Enterprise IG**
Design team	**Franco Bonadio, Martin Roche**
Graphics	**Jupiter Display**
Realisation	**Michael Whiteley Associates**
Size	**24 m²**
Photos	**Boots O'Leary**

Frames in Space

Rahmen im Raum

Burkhardt Leitner constructiv
own stand

Burkhardt Leitner constructiv
Eigenstand

Constructivism is the toko-no-ma of Modernism, like the central cool point of a Japanese house. Constructivism assumes that clarity, materials and order can create beauty. A beauty that is like classical typography, transparent. That is to say it should not interfere with the content. So the toko no ma is also a frame in space for objects of value or importance.

The stand designs of Burkhardt Leitner constructiv use visually minimal elements, but the quality of their conception and finish is in itself a design statement. At Euroshop 1999 they showed their CLIC and PILA Petite ranges, in a custom designed event called Eurotunnel, a felt passage across the aisle that linked two stands each using one of the ranges. A simple and elegant concept that won a Gold iF Award.

Konstruktivismus ist das toko-no-ma der Moderne, gleich dem zentralen, kühlen Punkt eines japanischen Hauses. Konstruktivismus geht davon aus, daß Klarheit, Materialien und Ordnung Schönheit erzeugen können. Eine Schönheit, die wie klassische Typographie transparent ist. Dadurch ist das toko-no-ma auch ein Rahmen im Raum für wertvolle oder wichtige Objekte.

Die Standentwürfe von Burkhardt Leitner constructiv verwenden sichtbar wenig Elemente, aber die Qualität ihres Konzepts und ihrer Ausführung ist eine Aussage über Design an sich. Auf der Euroshop 1999 präsentierten sie ihre Messe- und Ausstellungssysteme CLIC und PILA Petite in einem speziellen Entwurf: Ein Filzweg, Eurotunnel genannt, verband über den Gang hinweg zwei Stände, auf denen jeweils eines der Systeme installiert war. Ein einfaches und elegantes Konzept, welches von dem if Exhibition Design Award mit Gold ausgezeichnet wurde.

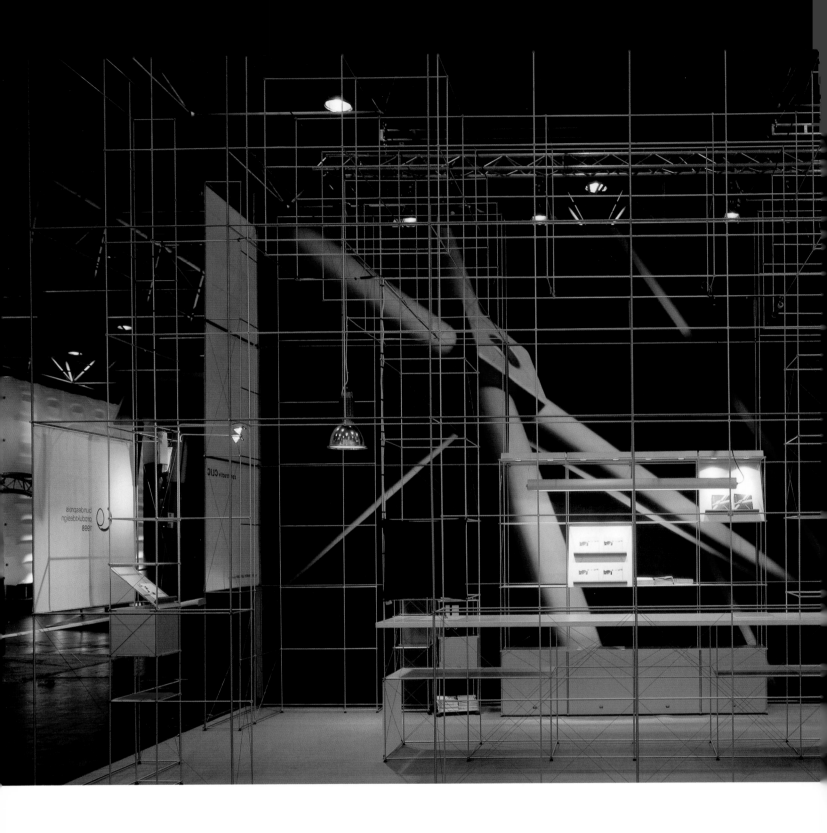

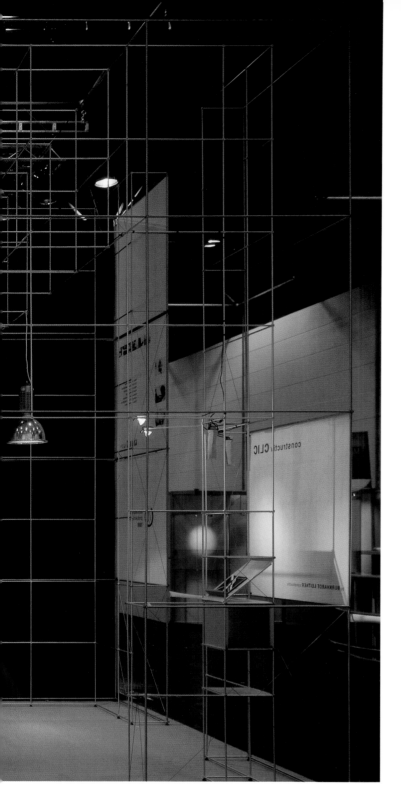

Most of their systems come in kit form, so that they can be adapted to different locations. Apart from their technical strengths, they are designed to be assembled easily, almost intuitively, using simple tools. Like, as Burkhardt Leitner says, "a nomad's tent, the prototype of all temporary structures, agile and efficient."

Die Systeme sind modular aufgebaut und können unterschiedlichen Raumanforderungen gerecht werden. Trotz ihrer technischen Stärke können sie leicht, fast intuitiv mit einfachem Werkzeug zusammengebaut werden – „wie ein Nomadenzelt", sagt Burkhardt Leitner, „dem Prototyp aller temporären Stukturen, beweglich und effektiv."

BURKHARDT LEITNER constructiv

beweglichkeit agility

Year	**1999**
Location	**Düsseldorf**
Trade Fair	**EuroShop**
Exhibitor	**Burkhardt Leitner constructiv GmbH & Co., Stuttgart**
Concept, Realisation	**Burkhardt Leitner constructiv GmbH & Co., Stuttgart**
Design team	**Michael Daubner, Team Burkhardt Leitner constructiv**
Graphics	**Fleischmann + Kirsch, Stuttgart**
Size	**138.5 m²**
Photos	**Bernd Kammerer**

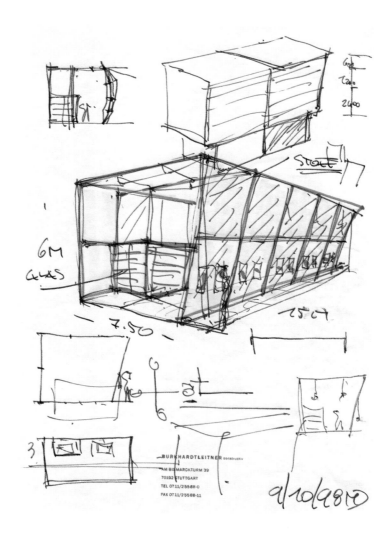

The Only Way is Up

Es kann nur aufwärts gehen

Exhibitgroup-Giltspur for
Fuji Medical Systems

Exhibitgroup-Giltspur für
Fuji Medical Systems

When you need more space in a busy fair, adding a further
level is often the only solution: how you do it is what counts.
Fuji Medical Systems had that problem at the RSNA show in
Chicago, and asked Alex Kaluzshner of Exhibitgroup-Giltspur
in New York to help them with that. Their previous design
had been a pair of deck structures surmounted by an illumi-
nated rice-paper covered cube. This was the only glowing
exhibit at the fair, and the client wanted it maintained - but
wanted a conference area as well.

Wer auf einer dicht gedrängten Messe mehr Platz benötigt, kann oft nur ein Stockwerk aufsetzen: Wichtig dabei
ist das Wie. Fuji Medical Systems hatte dieses Problem auf
der RSNA in Chicago und bat Alex Kaluzshner von Exhibitgroup-Giltspur in New York um Hilfe. Ihr vorheriges Design
hatte aus zwei Decks bestanden, die von einem beleuchteten
Kubus aus Reispapier gekrönt wurden. Es war der einzige
Messestand, der leuchtete, und der Kunde wollte das Konzept beibehalten – aber einen Besprechungsraum hinzufü-
gen.

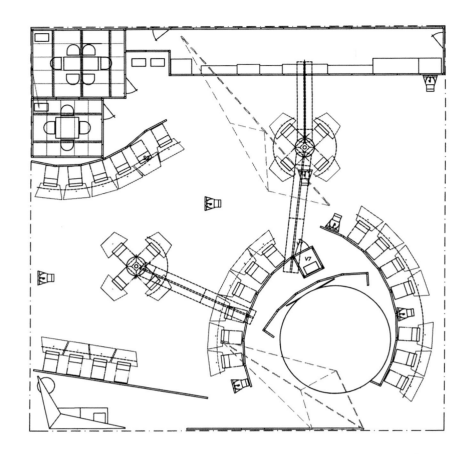

The answer was to place the conference area within a truncated pyramid projecting out from the main deck and lit from the underside. The pyramidal form was dramatic in itself, and took advantage of the rule that stands had to begin four feet in from the aisle at ground level, but could project to the aisle at a higher level. The pyramid theme was repeated in the interior with a smaller, internally-lit pyramid descending from the roof.

The final design has an architectonic quality that retains and refines the original concept to make a landmark stand. The aim, Kaluzshner says, was to captivate and elevate the visitor: "You feel how important you are to Fuji: They took care of you; they brought you to this upscale space."

Die Lösung bestand darin, den Besprechungsraum innerhalb einer abgeflachten Pyramide zu plazieren, die, von unten beleuchtet, vom Hauptdeck vorsprang. Die Pyramidenform an sich war dramatisch und nutzte die Vorgabe, daß Stände ebenerdig 120 cm vom Gang entfernt sein mußten, auf einer höheren Ebene aber in den Gang hinausragen durften. Das Thema „Pyramide" wiederholt sich im Innern des Stands mit einer kleineren, von innen beleuchteten Pyramide.

Das abgeschlossene Design hat eine architektonische Qualität, die das ursprüngliche Konzept bewahrt und optimiert, ein Wahrzeichen schafft. Ziel war es, sagt Kaluzshner, den Besucher zu fesseln und ihm ein gutes Gefühl zu vermitteln: „Man spürt wie wichtig man für Fuji ist."

Year	**1998/1999**
Location	**Chicago**
Trade Fair	**RSNA-Radiological Society of North America**
Exhibitor	**Fuji Medical Systems USA Inc.**
Concept	**Exhibitgroup-Giltspur, New York Region**
Design	**Alex Kaluzshner – Lead Designer, Creative Director, Joseph Arico – Designer, Computer Modeling**
Realisation	**Exhibitgroup-Giltspur, New York Region**
Size	**605 m²**
Photos	**Padjett and Company**

Siemens
Design
&Messe
GmbH

Inflated Opportunities

Unendliche Dehnungen

Siemens Design & Messe
own stand

Siemens Design & Messe
Eigenstand

At most fairs, stands are there for the client companies, each one an individual statement in the matrix of the whole. But if your business is exhibition organisation and stand design, how do you place yourselves? Siemens Design & Messe found a light-hearted but serious response to this for Euroshop 1999.

Chefs on the ground floor, chiefs on the balcony: a small rectangular stand with an upper level overhang, meaning relaxing space for meetings around tables at floor level, or serious talk upstairs. Perhaps, but the enticing part of the design lies in the exterior walls.

Die meisten Messestände werden von Designern für Kunden entworfen. Jeder davon hat eine individuelle Aussage, die sich nach dem Marketingkonzept des Kunden richtet. Wenn man aber selbst professionell Ausstellungen organisiert und Stände entwirft, wie präsentiert man sich dann? Siemens Design & Messe hat für die Euroshop 1999 eine unbeschwerte, aber trotzdem ernstzunehmende Antwort gefunden.

Ebenerdig die Besucher, auf dem „Balkon" die Entscheider. Ein kleiner, rechteckiger Stand mit einem Überhang im oberen Stockwerk: Der untere Teil ist für entspannte Gespräche an runden Tischen gedacht, der obere für wichtige Meetings. Der verführerischste Aspekt dieses Standdesigns liegt jedoch in seinen Außenwänden.

These consist of strips of inflated pod sections hung from the ceiling frame to ground level. On the exterior, they present a formal but unexpected definition of the presence of the stand, as if when things got too busy they could bulge conveniently outwards. Normally they soften the lighting, creating a warm and inviting atmosphere in which to do fair business, around their message to the trade fair world "Competence and Innovation in Design and Event Management."

Streifen aufgeblasener Hülsen, die vom Deckenrahmen bis auf den Boden hängen, bilden die Außenwand. Sie geben dem Stand eine äußerst präsente Anmutung, als könne er sich jederzeit ausdehnen, wölben und seinem geschäftigen Innenleben anpassen. Aufgabe dieser Hülsen ist es zudem, das Licht zu dämpfen und eine warme, einladende Atmosphäre zu schaffen, in der es leicht fällt, fair und freundlich Geschäfte abzuschließen. Die Botschaft an die Messewelt lautete: „Kompetenz und Innovation in Design- und Eventmanagement".

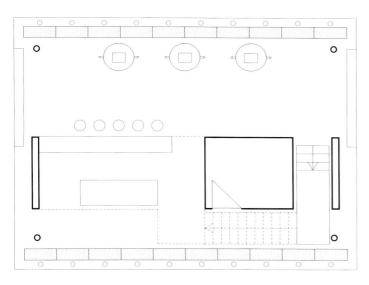

Year	**1999**
Location	**Düsseldorf**
Trade Fair	**EuroShop**
Exhibitor	**Siemens Design & Messe GmbH**
Concept	**Siemens Design & Messe GmbH: Stefan Amschler, Ulrich Kostka**
Realisation	**Siemens Design & Messe GmbH**
Size	**88 m²**
Photos	**Siemens Design & Messe GmbH**

International Council of Shopping Centers 1999

Cruising the Mall

Lust am Einkaufen

Lorenc + Yoo Design for
First Union

Lorenc + Yoo Design für
First Union

Change of ownership is often a reason for redesigns, from management structures and corporate identities through to trade fair stands. When the property and leasing company First Union Investment came into new hands, the owners felt they should demonstrate their commitment to the retail sector by creating a new stand for the ICSC show in Las Vegas.

Lorenc Yoo Design felt that the appropriate architectural metaphor for the client's position was what they termed "Modern Classic," suggesting that the idea of the contemporary mall goes back to the agora or marketplace of Ancient Greece. Visitors were invited to walk through a mini-mall with "shop windows" full of goods and with graphic panels setting our First Union's history and values.

Ein neuer Besitzer bringt oft auch neue Konzepte, angefangen bei Management Strukturen über Corporate Identities bis hin zu Messeständen. Als die Property- and Leasing-Gesellschaft First Union Investment den Besitzer wechselte, sollte als Zeichen des Engagements gegenüber dem Verkaufssektor für die ICSC Messe in Las Vegas ein neuer Stand entworfen werden.

Lorenc Yoo Design war der Meinung, das passende architektonische Symbol für die Position des Kunden sei „Modern Classic". Dieser Vorschlag geht darauf zurück, daß das Konzept des zeitgenössischen Einkaufzentrums auf der „Agora", dem Marktplatz im antiken Griechenland basiert. Besucher wurden eingeladen zu einem Bummel durch ein Mini-Einkaufszentrum mit „Schaufenstern" und Stellwänden, auf denen Historie und Wertvorstellungen von First Union grafisch dargestellt waren.

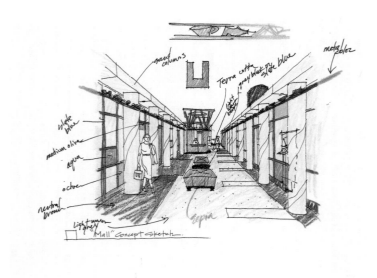

The result is a postmodern fantasy, with painted columns and Pompeian red booths. Rich in colour and detail, the stand communicates an enthusiastic belief in shopping style, and marked out First Union as a brand with its eye on the future.

Das Ergebnis ist eine postmoderne Phantasiewelt mit bemalten Säulen und antik-roten Marktständen. Reich an Farbe und Detail, vermittelt der Stand den begeisterten Glauben an den Stil der Handelspartner und präsentiert First Union als eine Marke mit dem Blick auf die Zukunft.

Year	**1999**
Location	**Las Vegas**
Trade Fair	**International Council of Shopping Centers (ICSC): Leasing Mall**
Exhibitor	**First Union Management, Cleveland, Ohio and New York**
Concept	**Lorenc + Yoo Design / Journey Communications, Roswell**
Design Team	**Jan Lorenc – Design Director / Project Manager, David Park – Designer, Steve McCall – Designer, Janice McCall – Interior Designer, Chung Youl Yoo – Designer Journey Communications: Beth Cochran**
Lighting	**Ramon Luminence Design: Ramon Noya**
Multi-media team	**Journey Communications – CD ROM Interactive presentation**
Graphics, Communication	**Lorenc + Yoo Design: Veda Sammy – Graphic Designer**
Realisation	**GeoGraph Industries, Cincinnati : George Freudiger**
Size	**approx. 1,220 m²**
Photos	**Rion Rizzo: Creative Sources Photography**

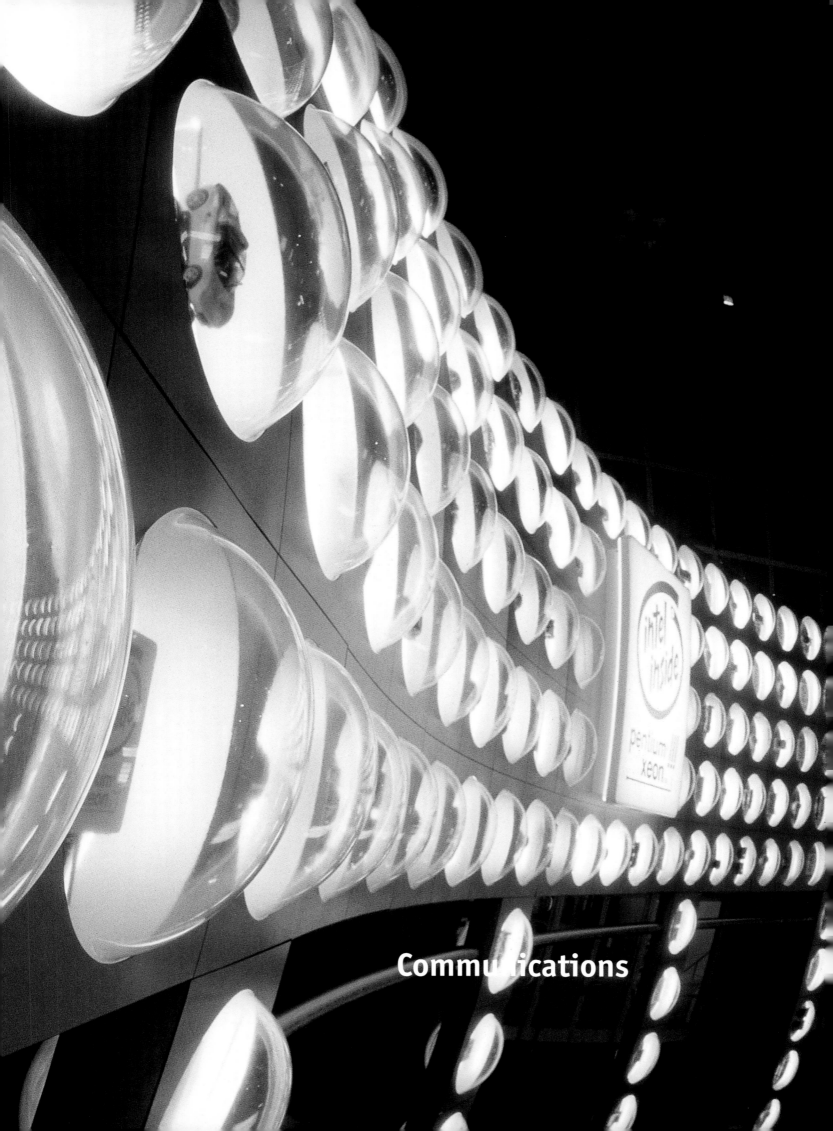

Communications

Getting Inside the Inside

Im Innern des Innern

Mauk Design
for Intel

Mauk Design
für Intel

We all know the strapline "Intel Inside." But how to deliver that message through the visual dynamics of a stand, and about an object a couple of centimetres across? Mauk Design, whom Intel commissioned for their stand for the 1999 Siggraph exhibit, chose to develop the theme of a theatre. But not, as others have done, by making the main presentation area the centre: it is at the back of the stand. Rather by using the concept of going to the theatre: the grand entrance, the wait in the foyer for seats, in other words by building anticipation and so interest.

The front corner of the stand is a an imposing curved portico, set with softly glowing bubbles containing models of the racing cars featured in Intel's advertising campaigns.

Wir alle kennen den Slogan „Intel Inside". Wie aber soll man diese Nachricht mittels der optischen Dynamik eines Stands und einem wenige Zentimeter großen Objekt übermitteln? Mauk Design, von Intel für den Stand auf der Siggraph 1999 beauftragt, wählte als Thema das Theater. Nicht indem sie, wie andere vor ihnen, die Hauptpräsentationsfläche in den Mittelpunkt stellten – sie ist im hinteren Teil des Stands. Sondern dadurch, daß sie das Konzept Theaterbesuch ausarbeiteten: Der großartige Eingang, das Warten im Foyer auf den Einlaß, in anderen Worten die Vorfreude und das so geweckte Interesse.

Die Vorderfront des Stands, ein imponierender, gewölbter Portikus, ist mit sanft leuchtenden Blasen bedeckt und zeigt Modelle der Rennwagen, welche in Intels Werbekampagne mitwirken.

These are set alongside new Xeon processors, both icons of speed. In the foyer area those waiting were entertained by images on a plasma totem pole, while six curved steel stanchions helped form lines in front of the theatre entrance itself.

This was headed with superimposed images of a human and robotic brain, and a series of television screens. Within the theatre, coloured in Intel's corporate blue, and carrying the show theme "Shorten the distance between thinking it and seeing it." After the wide screen presentation, the audience was invited to try the new products at a series of demonstration stands or to view the technology presentation wall. The desks in the demo stations were in translucent underlit resin, embedded with floating chips. There were two adjacent smaller presentation areas on each side of the main theatre.

This approach not only turns presentation theatre into drama, both from outside the stand and within, it also handles successfully a high throughput of visitors in the fairly tight space of a seventy by eighty foot stand. The overall effect is conveyed through the depth of detail: the technology showcase is a bubble wall that deliberately recalls the entrance wall, though in a different colour theme, and the lit vacuum-formed bubbles give presence to the circuit boards displayed inside them. Circuit board patterns are also used as wallcoverings for the theatre entrance side-walls. The curves of the entrance stanchions are matched by the curved chairs selected for the secondary presentation areas, and by the shapes of the demonstration desks. And so on.

Circuit boards and processors have no product semantics: nothing in their appearance shows their function. Showing and explaining such objects requires presentation techniques, as everyone knows. The skill and subtlety of this stand lies in its ability to make the presentation an event, not just a necessity.

Sie sind entlang neuer Xeon Prozessoren aufgebaut, beides Ikonen der Geschwindigkeit. Die Wartenden im Foyer werden mit Bildern auf einem Plasma-Totempfahl unterhalten, während sechs gebogene Stahlgeländer die Menschenschlange vor dem Theatereingang leiten.

Dieser wurde gekrönt von projizierten Bildern eines Menschen-, eines Roboterhirns und einer Reihe von Fernsehbildschirmen. Im Theater, ganz im Intel-Firmenblau gehalten, der Messeslogan: „Shorten the distance between thinking it and seeing it." Nach der Präsentation auf der Breitleinwand wurde das Publikum ermutigt, die neuen Produkte an einer Reihe von Displays auszuprobieren oder die neuen Technologien zu begutachten. Die Pulte in den Displays waren aus durchsichtigem, von innen beleuchtetem Kunstharz mit eingebetteten Chips. Entlang den Seiten des Haupttheaters gab es noch je zwei zusammenhängende, kleinere Präsentationsflächen.

Auf diese Art wird nicht nur Präsentationstheater in Drama verwandelt, sondern auch ein hohes Quantum an Publikumsverkehr durch den verhältnismäßig engen Stand von 21 auf 24 Metern geführt. Der Gesamtauftritt vermittelt Liebe zum Detail: Der Technologie-Schaukasten ist eine Blasenwand, die, trotz einer anderen Farbgebung, eindeutig an die Vorderfront des Stands erinnert. Die darin ausgestellten Leiterplatten erhalten durch die beleuchteten, vakuumgeformten Blasen Präsenz. Leiterplattenmuster bedecken auch die Seitenwände des Theatereingangs. Die Kurven des Eingang-Geländers werden aufgegriffen von den Kurven der Stühle im kleineren Präsentationsbereichs und von der Form der Demonstrationspulte.

Leiterplatten und Prozessoren sind als Produkt nicht formulierbar: Ihre Funktion wird durch nichts in ihrem Äußeren erklärt. Solche Objekte zu zeigen und zu erklären erfordert, wie jeder weiß, Präsentationstechniken. Geschick und Finesse dieses Stands liegen in seiner Fähigkeit, die Präsentation zu einem Ereignis zu machen, nicht nur zu einer Notwendigkeit.

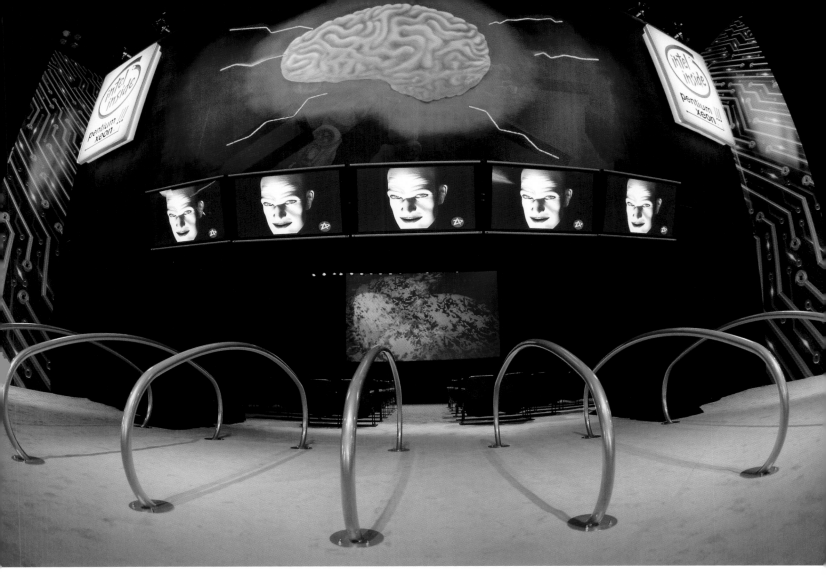

Left: CAD visualisation of
the completed design.

Above: The entrance to the
presentation area shows a
continuous video display to
waiting visitors, under a
morphing image of a brain.

Links: CAD-Visualisierung
des Aufbaus

Oben: Der Eingang zum
Präsentationsbereich zeigt
eine Video-Leinwand für
wartende Besucher.

Year	**1999**
Location	**Los Angeles**
Trade Fair	**Siggraph**
Exhibitor	**Intel Corporation**
Concept	**Mauk Design**
Design team	**Mitchell Mauk, Laurence Raines**
Multi-media team	**Delphi Productions**
Realisation	**Exhibitgroup-Giltspur, San Francisco**
Size	**approx. 870 m²**
Photos	**Andy Caulfield**

Flying the Flag

Flagge zeigen

Interbrand Zintzmeyer & Lux for
Deutsche Telekom

Interbrand Zintzmeyer & Lux für
Deutsche Telekom

"A graphic representation of data extracted from the banks of every computer in the human system. Unthinkable complexity. Lines of light ranged in the nonspace of the mind." William Gibson's description of cyberspace, from his novel Neuromancer (the book that coined the concept) could well be the starting metaphor for the Deutsche Telecom stand at CeBIT.

CeBIT is a major international show, and Deutsche Telecom the national network of the host country. They asked identity specialists Interbrand Zintzmeyer & Lux to design a stand with "total command of the event," a term they had used for their IFA '97 exhibit from the same design team.

„Eine grafische Darstellung der Daten aus der Datenbank jedes Computers im menschlichen System. Unvorstellbare Komplexität. Lichtlinien erstrecken sich über den Nichtraum des Geistes." William Gibsons Beschreibung des Cyberspace aus seinem Buch „Neuromancer" (jenem Buch, welches das Konzept prägte) könnte gut die ursprüngliche Metapher für den Stand der Deutschen Telekom auf der CeBIT sein. Die CeBIT ist eine wichtige internationale Messe, die Deutsche Telekom der wichtigste Netzanbieter des Gastlandes. Sie beauftragten die Identity-Spezialisten Interbrand, Zintzmeyer & Lux einen Stand zu entwerfen, der „die Messe beherrschen sollte"– ein Begriff den sie bereits mit denselben Standarchitekten auf der IFA '97 verwendet hatten.

Coloured light-tubes as a
network

Farbige Neonröhren bilden
ein Netzwerk

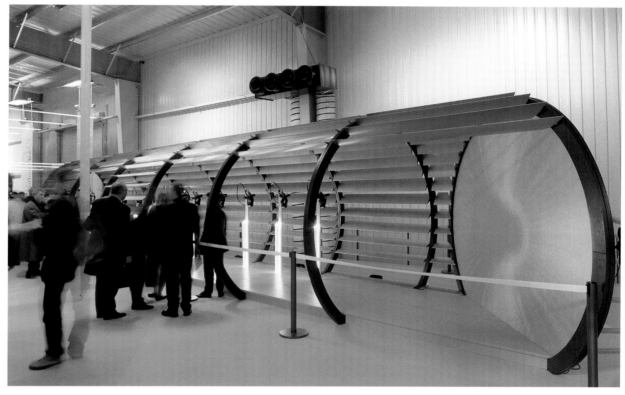

The design solution was to use the airspace above the stand as a network, filled with lines of coloured light-tubes. This matrix represented the connectivity between different media and the future-oriented approach central to the client's position. Additional themes were pinpointed on vertical banners over the glass-walled meeting areas of the stand. This transparency was also deliberate, underpinning the themes of accessibility and offer.

Die Lösung bestand darin, den Freiraum über dem Stand mit farbigen Neonröhren zu füllen, die als Netzwerk fungierten. Dadurch wurde die Verbindung von unterschiedlichen Medien mit dem zukunftsorientierten Ansatz des Kunden versinnbildlicht. Zusätzliche Themen wurden auf vertikalen Stoffbahnen festgehalten, die über den Glaswänden um die Meeting-Nischen des Standes hingen. Diese Transparenz war durchaus beabsichtigt, um die Themen Zugänglichkeit und Angebot zu unterstreichen.

Year	**1999**
Location	**Hanover**
Trade Fair	**CeBIT**
Exhibitor	**Deutsche Telekom AG**
Concept	**Interbrand Zintzmeyer & Lux AG, Zurich**
Architectural Planning	**Büro Manfred Kruska**
Media	**TC-Gruppe, Ludwigsburg**
Lighting Company	**Sound & Light Veranstaltungstechnik GmbH, Leonberg**
Sound- & AV-Company	**Sound & Light Audiovisions GmbH, Leonberg**
Realisation	**Holtmann Messebau, Ingenieurbau**
Size	**3,000 m²**
Photos	**avcommunication: Frank Erber**

Storing the Future

Die Zukunft speichern

Thinc Design for Seagate

Thinc Design für Seagate

Seagate were among the pioneers of commercial hard drives, essential for computer users, ever hungry for more and faster data storage. But Seagate devices live hidden inside computers. Communicating their functions is the key to presentation.

For the 1999 Comdex stand, Thinc Design (the name is a contraction of the founder's name, Tom Hennes, plus Incorporated) set out a number of user needs for which Seagate products were the solution. "Information the way you want it' and "Enterprise information management" for example. These were under a general theme of "see storage differently." The needs were set out on triangular banners hung from pylons at the edge of the stand to the central round meeting room. This seemingly abstract design is also a visual echo of the pattern of discs and reader arms within a hard drive.

Seagate ist einer der Pionier-Anbieter für kommerzielle Festplatten – wichtig für Nutzer, die nach größeren und schnelleren Datenspeichern hungern. Weil diese Festplatten aber versteckt im Innern eines Computers sind, liegt der Schlüssel zur Präsentation in der Vermittlung ihrer Funktion.

Für den Comdex Stand 1999 stellte Thinc Design (der Name setzt sich aus den Initialen des Gründers Tom Hennes plus Incorporated zusammen) einige Nutzer-Bedürfnisse zusammen, für die Seagate-Produkte die Lösung darstellen: z.B. „Information, wie sie gewünscht wird" und „Unternehmen Information Management" – das alles gesammelt unter dem allgemeinen Thema „Speichern, mal anders gesehen". Die Bedürfnisse wurden auf dreieckige Fahnen gedruckt, die an Masten vom Rand des Standes bis zum runden Konferenzzimmer in der Mitte hingen. Dieser scheinbar abstrakte Entwurf geht auf ein konkretes Bild zurück: es nimmt das Muster von Disketten und Lesearmen innerhalb einer Festplatte auf.

enterprise
information
management

Seagate

newly announced
products

Seagate

newly announced
products

This is a neat solution: what gives it an edge is the use of projectors to overlay images and patterns on the banners, pylons and building of the stand. The changing colours and shapes of the lightshow mirror the passage of data through a computer. Hardware into lightware, perhaps.

Eine saubere Lösung: Der Einsatz von Projektoren, um Bilder und Muster auf die Fahnen, die Masten und das Standgebäude werfen zu können, gibt dem Ganzen den speziellen Touch. Die wechselnden Farben und Formen der Lichtshow spiegeln den Weg der Daten durch den Computer wieder. Von der Festplatte zum Lichterfest?

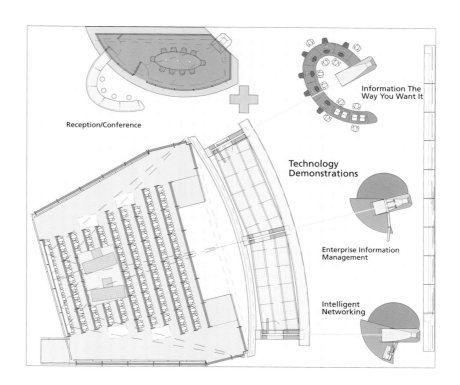

Reception/Conference

Information The Way You Want It

Technology Demonstrations

Enterprise Information Management

Intelligent Networking

Year	**1998**
Location	**Las Vegas**
Trade Fair	**Comdex**
Exhibitor	**Seagate Technology, Inc.**
Concept	**Thinc Design, New York**
Design team	**Tom Hennes, Dana Christensen, Jim Goldschmidt, Rick Stockton**
Lighting	**Paul Palazzo**
Graphics	**Drive Communications**
Communication	**Clarity** **Realisation: Exhibitree, Irvine**
Realisation	**Exhibitree, Irvine**
Size	**606 m²**
Photos	**Jaime Padgett**

Lucent Technologies
Bell Labs Innovations

Managing Network Complexity

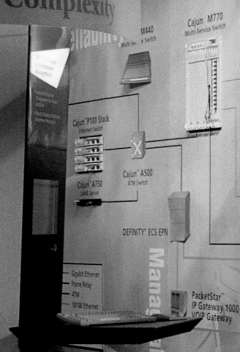

Modular Communications
Modulare Kommunikation

Exhibitgroup-Giltspur for
Lucent Technologies

Exhibitgroup-Giltspur für
Lucent Technologies

Lucent Technologies are market leaders in the US (and worldwide) telecommunications industry. They wanted a new design that would convey this message, and also specified that the design be modular, for while it would be unveiled at the 1999 Comnet show in Washington, it would also be used, in different configurations, elsewhere.

The designer, Midi Kim, went back to basic geometry to develop the concept. A circle and a triangle are the main elements: the circle happily echoes Lucent's own brushstroke logo, while the triangle can be read as a metaphor for cutting edge technology. The triangle also governs the wedge shapes of the product stations that are an important and integral part of the stand. These have sufficient physical presence while not overwhelming the individual products they display, and their form, though repeated, is not dull.

Lucent Technologies sind in den USA (und weltweit) marktführend innerhalb der Telekommunikationsindustrie. Um diese Information zu vermitteln, beauftragten sie ein neues, modulares Design. Es sollte zwar auf der Comnet 1999 in Washington enthüllt, aber auch anderswo, in anderer Gestalt, eingesetzt werden können.

Der Designer Midi Kim besann sich auf einfache Geometrie, um das Konzept zu entwickeln. Ein Kreis und ein Dreieck sind die Hauptelemente: Der Kreis erinnert auf fröhliche Weise an Lucents eigenes, gepinseltes Logo, während das Dreieck als Symbol für die Schärfe der Technologie interpretiert werden kann. Das Dreieck bestimmt auch die Keilform der Produktstationen, welche ein wesentlicher und zentraler Bestandteil des Stands sind. Kreis und Dreieck haben ausreichend Präsenz, ohne die einzelnen ausgestellten Produkte zu überwältigen, und ihre Form ist, trotz der Wiederholung, nicht langweilig.

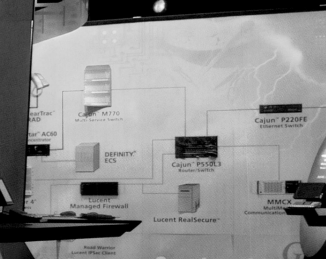

High-powered "Cajun Campus" Network

Lucent Technologies

Automated IP Services Management

- High Performance DNS/DHCP Servers
- Fault Intolerant Architecture
- LDAPv3/Directory Services Support

Cajun M770 ATM

- Premier Enterprise-Class ATM Multi-function Switch for Reliable Support of Converging Networks
- Fault Tolerant Platform for Mission-critical ATM Backbone and Ethernet Applications

Cajun P580 ATM Switch & ATM/LAN Packet Server

- 40/80 Mid-sized ATM Switch Supporting Voice, Data, and Video Convergence
- ATM Industry-leading LANE and MPOA Server Capabilities 50 to 200K BGL Performance

ClearTrac RAD

Cajun M770
Multi-Service Switch

Cajun P220FE
Ethernet Switch

AC60
Concentrator

DEFINITY ECS

Cajun P550L3
Router/Switch

MMCX
MultiMedia
Communications

Lucent
Managed Firewall

Lucent RealSecure

Road Warrior
Lucent IPSec Client

Serviceability

The product station could be grouped with others, and, for example, linked by a circle or arc band above, or stand in backed pairs, thus creating the required flexibility for different show setups.

The base colours used on the stand are based on Lucent's own off-white corporate colours. Dramatic lighting effects were therefore incorporated to add contrast and excitement, with the contrasts becoming stronger as the visitor moved further into the stand. The simple range of forms combines with the density of the technology on offer to create a vibrant and satisfying solution.

Die Produktstationen können als Gruppe auftreten und z.B. von einem sie überspannenden Kreis oder Bogen zusammengehalten werden, oder als Paar Rücken an Rücken stehen. Dadurch haben sie die für verschiedene Messesituationen erforderliche Flexibilität.

Die Basisfarben des Stands beruhen auf Lucents eigenen rohweißen Firmenfarben. Dramatische Lichteffekte wurden eingebaut, um Kontrast und Spannung zu schaffen, wobei der Kontrast sich auf dem Weg ins Innere des Stands verstärkt. Die Auswahl einfacher Formen, kombiniert mit der Dichte der ausgestellten Technologie, schafft eine lebendige und befriedigende Lösung.

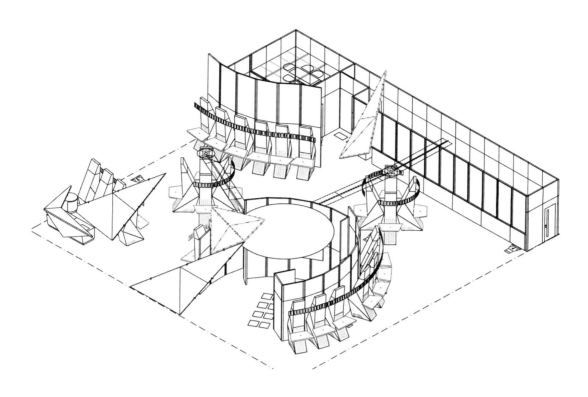

Year	**1999**
Location	**Washington**
Trade Fair	**Comnet**
Exhibitor	**Lucent Technologies, Muray Hill, NJ**
Concept	**Exhibitgroup-Giltspur** **New York Region**
Design team	**Midi Kim – Lead Designer,** **Kelly Schlenker – Graphic Designer**
Realisation	**Exhibitgroup-Giltspur** **New York Region**
Size	**330 m²**
Photos	**Padjett and Company**

Homepages

Arno Design, Munich
www.arno-design.de
email: office@arno-design.de

Bürling Schindler Freie Architekten BDA, Stuttgart
email: buerlingschindler@csi.com

d'art Design Gruppe, Neuss
www.D-Art-Design.De
email: info@D-Art-Design.De

Dietrich Display, Friolzheim
www.dietrichdisplay.de
email: dietrichdisplay@t-online.de

Enterprise IG, London
www.enterpriseig.com
email: info@enterpriseig.com

Exhibitgroup Giltspur, Edison (NJ)
www.e-g.com.

Imagination Ltd, London
www.imagination.com

Ingenhoven Overdiek und Partner
Kaistr. 16A
D-40221 Düsseldorf

Interbrand Zintzmeyer & Lux, Zurich
www.interbrand.ch
email: contact@interbrand.ch

Kauffmann Theilig & Partner, Ostfildern
email: architekten.ktp@t-online.de

Prof. Wolfgang Körber, Solingen
email: wkoerb1219@AOL.com

Burkhardt Leitner constructiv, Stuttgart
www.burkhardtleitner.de
email: info@ burkhardtleitner.de

lorenc yoo design
www.lorencyoodesign.com
email: jan@lorencyoodesign.com

Mauk Design, San Francisco
www.maukdesign.com
email: info@maukdesign.com

McMillanGroup
www.mcmillangroup.com

meiré und meiré, Frechen/Königsdorf
www.meireundmeire.de
email: 100124.2066@compuserve.com

Architectures Jean Nouvel
10, Cité d'Angoulême
F-75011 Paris

root., London
email: root.@easynet.co.uk

Oliver Schrott Kommunikation, Cologne
www.osk.de
email: osk@osk.de

Siemens Design & Messe GmbH, Erlangen
www.siemensdesign.de
email: info@siemens-d-m.de

Dieter Thiel
Maiengasse 1
CH- 4056 Basel

Thinc Design, New York
www.thincdesign.com
email: mail@thincdesign.com

Zumtobel Staff, Dornbirn
www.zumtobelstaff.co.at
email: info@zumtobelstaff.co.at

Author's thanks

The transient realities of trade fair design have always inter-
ested me, and the invitation to continue Karin Schulte's fine
work on the 1999 Yearbook was an honour. Special thanks
go to Petra, Eva and the others at **av**edition for their enthusi-
asm and support.

   This project was carried forward very much by the enthusi-
asm of the designers themselves for it, and my thanks go to
all of them. Among them my particular thanks go to Adrian
Caddy, Mitchell Mauk and Martin Root, as also to Holly
Browne, Anna Hastings, Tom Hennes, Charlotte Kruk, Jan
Lorenc, Burkhardt Leitner, Sylvia Olp, and Jocelyn Senior.

Die Vergänglichkeit des Messedesigns hat mich schon immer
interessiert. Es war mir eine Ehre, die Einladung anzunehmen,
Karin Schultes wunderbare Arbeit für das Jahrbuch 1999 fort-
zusetzen. Besonderer Dank geht an Petra und Eva und die
anderen bei der **av**edition für ihre Begeisterung und ihre
Unterstützung.

   Vorangetrieben wurde dieses Projekt vor allem durch die
Begeisterung der Designer selbst, und ich danke jedem ein-
zelnen von ihnen. Unter ihnen geht mein spezieller Dank an
Adrian Caddy, Mitchell Mauk und Martin Root, ebenso an
Holly Browne, Anna Hastings, Tom Hennes, Charlotte Kruk,
Jan Lorenc, Burkhardt Leitner, Sylvia Olp und Jocelyn Senior.

Conway Lloyd Morgan

Dank / Note of thanks

The publisher and author wish to thank those companies, architects, agencies and photographers who have provided images and material and who have contributed towards the printing costs.

We would like to extend our particular thanks to Ambrosius Messebau, Frankfurt am Main, DaimlerChrysler AG, Stuttgart (Marketing Kommunikation PKW / Begegnungskommunikation) and Sound & Light, Leonberg.

Verlag und Autor danken den beteiligten Firmen, Architekten, Agenturen und Fotografen für die zur Verfügung gestellten Bilder, Materialien und Druckkostenzuschüsse.

Besonderer Dank für die freundliche Unterstützung gilt Ambrosius Messebau, Frankfurt am Main, DaimlerChrysler AG, Stuttgart (Marketing Kommunikation PKW / Begegnungskommunikation) und Sound & Light, Leonberg.

Imprint

Editors: Eva Wittwer
                    Petra Kiedaisch
                    Vineeta Manglani
Translation: Christiane Sherman
Design: Conway Lloyd Morgan
                    avcommunication GmbH
                    Julia Kleiner
Cover illustration: H. G. Esch, Trade Fair stand for Audi
Lithography: **av**communication GmbH
                    Corinna Rieber
Production: **av**communication GmbH
                    Gunther Heeb
Printed by: Leibfarth + Schwarz, Dettingen/Erms
Paper: Luxo Satin

Printed in Germany

ISBN 3-929638-36-3

Impressum

Redaktion: Eva Wittwer
                    Petra Kiedaisch
                    Vineeta Manglani
Übersetzung: Christiane Sherman
Gestaltung: Conway Lloyd Morgan
                    avcommunication GmbH
                    Julia Kleiner
Umschlagfoto: H. G. Esch: Audi-Messeauftritt
Lithographie: **av**communication GmbH
                    Corinna Rieber
Produktion: **av**communication GmbH
                    Gunther Heeb
Druck: Leibfarth + Schwarz, Dettingen/Erms
Papier: Luxo Satin

Printed in Germany

ISBN 3-929638-36-3